INTRODUCTION

"Don't Volunteer" may be the most important book anyone could ever read. On these pages the author, Jay Evenson, reveals his keen insight and warns about the tricks and dangers inherent in the legal environment in which we live. The book provides explicit advise on how government and big business play a multitude of scams and word games to manipulate and control the people.

Jay Evenson and I go back over 40 years during which time I have always been amazed as I read his editorials, articles and commentaries about the many problems facing the people and their system of governance. Too often his information is prophetic as it seems to take society and government 15 or 20 years to act on his revelations and recommendations.

I not only endorse this book, I urge everyone to take full advantage of the insights and warnings it contains - and suggest all family members and friends be made aware of this book - and read it!.

Boye Lafayette De Mente

Boyé Lafayette De Mente is the author of more than 70 books on the role of cultures and languages in the mindset and behavior of people—on why and how they submit themselves to environments that range from irrational and destructive to inhuman. To see a list and synopses of his books go to

www.authorsonlinebookshop.com

ABOUT JAY EVENSON

Jay has been in the newspaper business most of his life as a reporter, columnist, editor and publisher of weekly newspapers, magazines and a syndicated feature service. He is the author of *"Break the Rules & Win"* and *"When all else fails...RTDD"* plus several small booklets - and now, ***"Don't Volunteer..."***

He has devoted much of his time to reading and understanding the nation's laws, courts and our Constitution. Although he has read more law than many attorneys, he is a writer of news and views and uses this knowledge to encourage government officials to adhere to the U.S. Constitution – and make the public aware of the tricks being played on them by the legal and regulatory double-talk of the politicians, bureaucrats and courts.

He has been active in politics, a legislative candidate, Chamber of Commerce President, organizer of citizen groups, a charter member of President Reagan's Presidential Transition Foundation and a member of IRE (Investigative Reporters & Editors). He is national director of Survival Force of America, dedicated to informing government officials, the media and public, when actions are weakening the Constitution and Laws.

Don't Volunteer...

Until You KNOW
How Government & Corporate
Tricks Are Used to Control You!

Jay Evenson

ISBN: 978-0-937507-07-0 Soft Cover
Library of Congress Catalog Card Number: *2014906245*

Printed in The United States of America

First Edition
10 9 8 7 6 5 4 3 2 1
Editorial Art - * Loyd Dolan
Cover Photo - iStock
Cover Design - Dale Gervais
Research - Richard Hanover

Published by COMPASS BOOKS/SFA
PO Drawer 9996
Phoenix, AZ 85068
www.SFAmerica.net

This book is dedicated to that very special lady who has encouraged me to keep up the good fight, and to all those others who gave of their time and talents to make this information available to the American people!

TABLE OF CONTENTS

AUTHOR'S PREFACE

After 25 years of writing editorials and columns I reviewed the material and realized that it all contained a lot of good and still current information about how the government and corporations were playing tricks on the American public - devious methods designed to diminish the Rights of the people, legally. In 1987, with some encouragement from a lady friend, I reluctantly wrote *"Break The Rules And Win."* I did numerous talk shows and traveled over 10,000 miles promoting that book and its content. The book reached some people and did do some specific good, causing changes that I can trace directly to the book. I exposed how the Federal government was playing a trick on all 50 states to coerce them to set speed limits at 55 mph under the threat of losing highway trust funds if they didn't comply. A lot of private property was saved from "condemnation" by developers and local government trickery.

Since then many government procedures and regulations have been changed. Urban renewal programs no longer exist by that name, but the bureaucrats and controllers have coined new phrases and gimmicks to accomplish the same ends. Although these tricksters found new ways to play similar scams on the people, many of their deceitful programs have been stopped.

Another 25 years have elapsed and I am now encouraged to give the world another book. Does the world really need another book? The answer is "Yes", but only if it can do some good and make things better!

Attempting to reveal how government and major businesses trick people to volunteer away their Rights is a daunting task. It becomes even more challenging when describing the various tricks used by the multitude of departments, boards, bureaus, authorities, administrations, courts, tribunals and agencies in a 250-page book.

"DON'T VOLUNTEER!" is intended for those who would prefer to stop standing on the sidelines waiting for their turn in the "screw the people" barrel. Some of the information in this

book is a continuum and update of *"Break The Rules And Win"* and is directed to people who know there is something amiss and grossly unfair in the administration of our justice system and government - people who want a reasonable way to protect themselves and, when possible, to fight back and win! The purpose is to point out to the readers how to identify the various tricks and tricksters so they can stop being a victim. The subjects and chapters encompass many facets of our government, with a focus on volunteering your Rights away, but it is all about government, big business and protecting your Unalienable Rights and property.

When I was much, much younger, I organized 300 cab drivers in El Paso, TX, as an association to fight discriminatory regulations by the city, police commissioner and others. The association members all paid minimal dues and when I went to pay a bill to the printer, he asked me, "Why are you doing this?"

I replied, "To help them!"

He looked at me pitifully *(I wasn't making any money)* and said, "Jesus Christ tried to help the people and they put him on a cross and crucified him. What makes you think you can do anything for them?"

I've always remembered that, but I can't seem to set-aside the motivation to help people who are being manipulated, controlled or oppressed by government!

Ronald Reagan often said "You can do a lot of good if you don't care who takes credit for it!"

I don't care who gets the credit for this information as long as things are changed for the better. If any reader of this book wants to run with the information, they don't even have to credit me, personally. However, the source (this book) should be referenced so others might be encouraged to read it and do something, too. There is always the possibility that the information and ideas this book promotes might be the little match that sparks a little fire that can turn into an outright blaze for liberty and justice!

Ergo, the world gets another book - **Don't Volunteer!**

Jay J. Evenson - April 2014

"Truth, knowledge, tolerance, vigilance –
all are required to preserve Liberty!"
– Jay Evenson

WARNING

You are well advised to seek counsel of a good lawyer when you need one, keeping in mind that the author is not a practicing attorney. Make sure that the lawyer you select is totally aware of this book and its content before allowing him or her to erroneously subject you to the questionable jurisdiction of an arbiter or court.

Don't Volunteer...

Until You KNOW

How Government & Corporate
Tricks Are Used to Control You!

**"THE FURTHER YOU LOOK BACK,
THE CLEARER YOU WILL SEE TODAY!"**

CHAPTER 1

BACK TO SQUARE ONE
Identify The Magicians' Tricks

If you think something is wrong with the way the government or some major company is functioning — chances are, you are right. If you find yourself the subject of bureaucratic harassment and you feel there is something wrong — chances are you are right!

Everyone has moments or even years in their past which they would like to undo or live over to avoid the actual - but unintended results. Kind of like going back to square one and reshaping our lives based on hindsight. But, alas, we don't have time travel machines and we usually have to live with our personal mistakes, adjust our plans and put forward our best efforts to move ahead. Hopefully, we make changes that will result in a better life for ourselves, our family and friends.

When our problems involve our government, laws, regulations and corporate entities we have to determine if the officials are just making uninformed mistakes or are they, and the special interest groups that manipulate them, actually looking for ways to circumvent the limitations imposed on them by our Constitution.

We want to point the finger at those who are responsible for this "something is wrong" syndrome. If we can't justifiably pin the blame on someone or some group we may eventually consider ourselves to be mere puppets in the scheme of things - or we become angry and start on an ineffective spiral of trying to do something. Too often we become discouraged and frustrated - we resign ourselves to the confused conditions! We Surrender!

But that isn't the answer! You and I are the "We", as in "We the people..."! We are responsible for allowing our personal affairs going astray and we are responsible if we allow our elected officials, legal system, courts and government to deviate from their originally authorized tasks. To find out how these manipulative magicians play their tricks requires going back to the start - *Square One!*

Just as it is difficult to pin-point the start of a family feud that has gone on for many years, such as the famous Hatfield and McCoy feud, it is even more challenging to search back to the beginning of an undesirable situation that exists within the laws, courts, regulations and procedures of our government. To do this we can't just critique or repeal the latest Act of Congress or pass another law to offset a court ruling and expect a different result. Most of the procedures that have allowed our system and our lives to be so confusing are very devious, but the trick they use is almost always revealed up front and it invariably involves "volunteering". The answers are right there for us to see if we look for them and know what to look for!

We are told early in life to always "read the fine print" and most of us follow that admonition. But we aren't looking at every word in the usually dull preamble to a contract, law or regulation. That is usually where we can find the start of our problems and it often involves a simple word or twisted phrase.

Some of what you will read may sound like "ancient history", but it is essential that people know how the problems started and how the tricks have been played in the past. Since the largest mass of regulations comes in the form of The Code of Federal Regulations (CFRs), which encompass over 240 volumes, you will be reading how numerous agencies of government play their tricks that often result in what many perceive to be a violation of their Rights. These are the rules the bureaucracy uses to spin a deceptive web – waiting to entrap you. Once you know how the tricks work, you can usually find ways to avoid the sticky webs. These rules are often touted as "the price we pay to live in a civilized society"! If you do decide to go-along with all the rules and regulations you must realize that you are doing so voluntarily and you really should stop complaining about losing your Rights! The U.S. Constitution is intact!

In subsequent chapters we are going to go back to *Square One* with brief but concise information regarding misleading court rulings, community development (HUD), black ops lobbyists, legislative procedures, insurance, licenses, Free Trade Agreements, corporate existence, banking scams, the Federal Reserve, funny money, the 16th Amendment (income tax), bureaucratic and political motivation, spin media, foreign influence, the abuse of words and phrases, the Code of Federal Regulations (CFR), legal trickery, the Holocaust and repeated special emphasis on how to avoid volunteering your Rights away. This repetition of "not volunteering" follows the theory that psychologists, educators and advertising agencies have successfully applied for decades – a person needs to be exposed to the message at least 13 times before they will have it ingrained in their memories. In the many examples of how different agencies play the same trick, you will read the admonition, "Don't Volunteer!" With the information in this book you will know how to identify the tricks and tricksters for yourself.

Don't misunderstand! Volunteering is your option! This information is not intended to encourage anarchy or rebellion - but to see that everyone knows the difference between rules (regulations) and actual laws that are necessary for living in a fair and civilized society. You can do it, or avoid it. But you must know that you are volunteering! If you go along and cooperate it may seem easier, but if you volunteer and don't question the controllers you qualify for life-time membership in the FOV – Fraternal Order of Victims!

Conquistadors Played The Trick!

A great example of how this volunteering trick has been played took place back in the 1600's when the Spanish Conquistadors enslaved the New World natives in Columbia and other areas in their quest for gold in the name of the King of Spain.

A Jesuit priest found that not only were the Aztec and Inca natives being enslaved, starved and murdered for minor infractions of the Spanish rules, they were not being taught about God and religion. This failure to provide them with soul-saving information was contrary to what the Catholic Church (a major force in

Spain) had required of the conquistadors on their adventures. The priest enlisted the aid of his superiors in the church and the King of Spain was notified about the lack of religious training. The King's lawyers immediately drafted a resolution to correct the problem.

The resolution, drafted in Latin and written on a magnificent rolled-up parchment scroll, was transported to the New World colonies where natives in each area were gathered together. Soldiers, armed with muskets stood at the ready, flags were flying and a drum roll grabbed the attention of everyone. Then the King's mandate was ceremoniously unrolled and read – in Latin – to the frightened natives.

The proclamation was simple enough: "If the native people will submit themselves for religious training they will no longer be treated as slaves. However, if you do not accept Christian training or you run away, you will be lawfully held as slaves to the King of Spain!"

At the end of the reading, the soldiers put their muskets on their shoulders, turned and marched away. The bewildered natives didn't understand a word of Latin and since the soldiers and guards marched away, they assumed that they had been set free! They immediately scattered into the surrounding jungles only to be pursued by the Spaniards who then took them as lawful slaves – as authorized by the Spanish King.

Variations of this trick continue to be played on Americans and other people around the world with legal terms, some also using Latin.

The perpetrators of the many scams played on people are not limited to the elected or appointed officials of government. Scam artists and conmen exist in every field, worldwide – law, medical, financial, farming, manufacturing, insurance, energy and the list goes on. But it isn't new! Similar tricks have been played on the public since the beginning of recorded history.

Some call the language used "legalese" and others call it "double-speak" or "gobble-de-gook". The obfuscating material is written in such a way that the average person, even most college graduates and lawyers, has difficulty grasping the differences and total meaning of the acts, laws, rules, codes, ordinances, regulations, decrees, treaties or contracts. When the procedure is based on a regulation based on a law that is based on a commonly accepted practice, the confusion is such that when you challenge the most recent regulation, the legal due process involved is so time consuming that two more rules, ordinances, regulations or laws have been applied and they still don't get back to the justification of the originating law.

This was the procedure used in Nazi Germany in the 1930's and 40's that led to World War II and the Holocaust. In Germany it was a bit faster and less sophisticated than it is applied today, but the same procedures and tricks are being used to control the people in the U.S. and other countries around the world. They really are doing it - AGAIN!

If you don't know where we have been, you will find it very difficult to move ahead without making the same mistakes! History does repeat itself, so when we want to fix what we consider wrong we have to understand how we got to where we are! People are "control conditioned" gradually. When the changes are gradual the public is often control-conditioned into accepting the current procedure or status as normal.

What can you do about it? Just find out and be aware of how the magicians play their tricks - and let everyone know. When the entire audience is familiar with the magicians' smoke and mirrors scams, they are less likely to pay to see the show.

TO PROVE A POINT

A great book suggested to prove a point about how big business can manipulate government at all levels to circumvent our Constitution and the will of the people, even in life and death situations, is *"Trading With the Enemy" by Charles Higham, Delacorte Press, N.Y.*

In it he reveals, via documents secured from our government under the Freedom Of Information Act (FOIA), that major banks, oil companies and other industries were exempted from the Trading With the Enemy Act, passed by Congress at the start of World War II. You will find that our own President, Franklin D. Roosevelt, signed a "General License" allowing American businesses to trade with the enemy under Executive Order No. 8389, just one week AFTER the Japanese attack on Pearl Harbor and Congress had officially declared war with Germany.

You will read how U.S. oil companies shipped fuel to their Argentina branches and then to Nazi submarines. You will learn that the Bank of England, as well as many American financiers, gleefully transferred funds to and from Nazi accounts while American, Canadian and British soldiers and sailors were being killed by the Germans.

Such firms as Standard Oil of New Jersey, the Chase Bank, the Texas Company, ITT and Ford Motor Company used the rules of war to trade with both sides.

Without going back to *Square One*, the information about business and government deals would not have been known.

SOMETHING FAMILIAR ABOUT THIS?

CHAPTER 2

NEVER AGAIN, AGAIN!
But It Is Happening... Again!

One of the bigger movements in the world is that promoted by Jewish organizations as they pledge "Never Again!" in reference to the Holocaust. It is a major effort to point to the horrible acts committed by the Nazis in Europe as they murdered over six million Jews and another 5 millions gypsies, homosexuals, mentally disturbed and other people Nazis considered "undesirable". But we, the American people, are allowing it to happen again! Despite the numerous displays, museums, media presentations and campaigns to remind the world of the Holocaust atrocities, something is missing – it virtually ignores the greatest of the atrocities - "how" it all started!

While visiting the U.S. Holocaust Museum when it first opened in Washington, DC, I was impressed to see a huge glass window display showing a rough chronological order of the many laws, decrees, rules, codes, ordinances, regulations and acts adopted by the Nazi government between 1930 and 1945. Those actions first required licensing and restricted movement. Then the Nazi rule-makers moved on to prohibit property ownership and certain occupations by specific undesirable minorities. Then the newly adopted codes were used to confiscate private property; then the teachers or other prohibited working persons were arrested and jailed; then definitions were given that deprived many of citizenship and even went to the point where they were declared sub-human ... and the murder of millions followed. For some reason the Holocaust Museum removed that particular display and I have tried repeatedly to find out where it went – to no avail. The curators are missing (or lost) that important element in describing the Holocaust.

But the Holocaust didn't just take place in Germany. As ordinary private citizens, the majority of German people were considered to be bystanders. They complied with the laws, rules, regulations and decrees without protest. For some it was just a matter of not admitting to themselves what was happening under the Nazi regime of terrorism. For others it was a matter of survival and, although they may have been consciously or unconsciously aware of the atrocities going on around them, they just wanted to get on with their everyday lives.

Poland, France, Austria, Holland, Norway and other countries the Nazi war machine invaded were also subject to application of the new decrees, rules, regulations and laws the conquering regime put into place.

Eventually there was resistance on the part of some citizens who recognized the threat to their very existence. Freedom Fighters and under-ground resistance groups were formed, so the Nazi commanders adopted even more regulations.

To make certain that farmers and villagers were not baking bread and feeding the resistance fighter, an official decree went out making it a death penalty offense to have possession of a small flour/wheat mill. Almost every farm home had one so the woman of the house could mill the wheat and bake bread. Without such mills the people were forced to buy their bread from the local bakers so the Nazis contollers could keep track of how much was purchased.

Again, some people just complied and went along with the Third Reich's edicts – until they finally realized that they, too, could wind up on a list for deportation to the work camps or death camps. Then they looked for guns with which to resist and fight back against the onslaught of the atrocities. But the first act of the Nazis when they invaded a nation was to disarm the population, making weapons difficult to secure for those who might think of resisting.

Some American do-gooders, our government, lawyers, banks and Wall Street firms are encouraging the same devious procedures to take control, make profits and deprive the American people of their Unalienable Rights.

A book describing how the Nazis took control via the legal and judicial system, *"The Law Under The Swastika"*, by Michael Stolleis, was written in 1998 and is now required reading at numerous major law schools in the U.S. But this raises the question: Are the soon-to-be lawyers being taught how to avoid and defend against similar laws and regulations or are they being taught how to play the tricks?

Don't Volunteer... *Don't Surrender!*

CHAPTER 3

THE DIFFERENCE
Regulations, Rules And Laws

Did you ever wonder how some people seem to be able to get away with almost anything, but if you even think of trying to do the same thing you are threatened with jail or some other legal problems?

In this age of computers, androids, cell phones and other high tech devices, people are often distracted from the devious changes in their government. To avoid being caught in a trap and labeled anti-social, an outlaw, terrorist or anarchist, everyone must know the difference between the regulations and laws. Laws are written to "protect" the people and their rights. Regulations are written to "control" the people and almost always limit their rights.

Do not confuse the U.S. Code (laws) with the Code of Federal Regulations (rules). You are required to obey the laws. You are not given options. Nobody can be exempt from a valid law. Valid laws are written within the limitations and restrictions imposed on government by our Constitution. Regulations cannot mandate obedience unless the purpose is to clarify a valid law - and you have voluntarily agreed or have been tricked into abiding by them.

Someone has been fighting city hall and they've been

winning! Pick up almost any daily newspaper or search your electronic news sources and you'll see an article or two about how some corporation or developer is "exempt" from obeying a certain law, or the law has been changed or ignored to accommodate a major industry.

The media is responsible for much of the misleading information. Editors (assuming their media's multi-national corporate owners will allow it) and journalism professors could solve part of the problem by teaching reporters to know the subtle but important differences between laws, regulations and policies.

Major companies, as well as wealthy, influential citizens seem to fight the bureaucracy and win. Occasionally we cheer silently when we hear stories of a little guy taking on the gigantic bureaucracy and coming out a winner. With a lump in our throat we again take pride in being free Americans, and we wish that we could fight such battles and win, too.

Big corporations have vast teams of lawyers, lobbyists and accountants going to bat for them. They seem to have virtually unlimited resources to use if some government agency resists their wishes. Railroads are given property tax breaks that make you wonder why their property should be taxed less than your home. You hear of public officials being caught with their hands in the cookie jar and they are merely transferred or fired from their job instead of going to trial and maybe prison. The big guys take their lawyers and drop-in on the Securities Exchange Commission (SEC) or some other agency and walk away with whatever exemption or exception they want.

How do these people get away with such actions and

get special considerations from the courts and the legal system? How can such firms apparently break the law and pay relatively small fines while the corporate officers go unpunished? You know what would happen to you if you tried the same thing... Jail! Right?

Those big firms are not being exempt from abiding by the law. They are excused from obeying certain regulations. That's the way things are. Don't you remember hearing about how "We must all obey the law!" or "No man is above the law!"? How about "Rules are made to be broken!" or "Rules are for simpletons!"? There is a difference in these old adages.

Nobody is or should be above the law! The Constitution clearly limits government authority and defines the authority that we, the people, have given to it. There are no exceptions to the law. It is simple, supposedly clear, and for everyone. But the procedures government uses to carry out its designated responsibilities are spelled out in the regulations, ordinances and rules. The regulations become mandatory on the part of government employees and they must obey them just as if the regulations are laws. If they don't like the rules, they can try to get them changed or they can go to work somewhere else.

Most companies adopt their own policies or rules of conduct by which their business is operated. The rules are enforced on the employees and penalties are exacted, such as docking an employee for being late or loss of certain privileges or position for failing to abide by the company policy. It is the right of the company to adopt reasonable rules and enforce them. If the employee does not want to abide by such rules, he or she can go elsewhere to work. The rules can even be discriminatory as long as they do not violate specific Federal laws against discrimination on the basis of sex, age, race or religious preference.

Most of us have certain rules we enforce in our own homes which, if used as "laws" outside the home, would be in violation of the Constitution and Rights of the people. We can make a rule that everyone who eats must wash the dishes. If you don't like the rule, don't sit down at the table. Within reason, you have the right to make such rules for your house and the government has the authority to legislate such rules and regulations for conducting its business.

However, the government usually passes regulations for its own agencies and employees to live and work by, and then the bureaucrats try to make their jobs easier by misconstruing the regulations as being enforceable against the general public, as if they are actual laws.

Back when Citizen Band (CB) radios became popular with truckers and motorists the Federal Communications Commission (FCC) had regulations that stated operators must have licenses and every CB radio must have a separate station license. To make public compliance easy, applications for station licenses were included along with the CB unit when it was purchased. The people continually refused to send them in to the FCC. Eventually, just to save face in the communications industry, FCC dropped the CB rules altogether.

The little guys resisted those rules and they won. Regulations are only given the force and effect of law if you volunteer (or are tricked into volunteering) for them. The regulations are often foisted first on major, highly regulated, businesses and industry that, by their existence, have volunteered to allow the rules and regulations to be imposed. Regulations and rules can only be enforced as law if the subjected parties agree or are tricked into complying with them.

The exception, which may not always be applicable, would be if the U.S. Senate ratified a treaty *(U.S. Constitution, Article VI)*, and the terms of that treaty then become the valid Law Of The Land - "the laws and constitutions of the States not withstanding." Such was the case when Limitations and Regulations were imposed on arms and ammunition manufacturers as the result of an International Arms Treaty *(Chapter 18)*. It was only supposed to prevent private firms and citizens from exporting weapons outside the U.S. without a government license. With such a Treaty becoming the law, bureaucrats, anti-gun activists and Congress joined together to force arms and weapons manufacturers to obey a new set of licensing regulations or they would not be permitted to export arms or munitions to foreign countries or sell them to the Pentagon. Those rules were then expanded and led to licensing of all firearms dealers, as buffers, who were then required to secure information from customers who were exercising their 2nd Amendment Right to keep and bear arms - virtual gun registration!

The U.S.-Canada Free Trade Agreement, and subsequently NAFTA and all other so-called free trade agreements, are examples of treaties being manipulated so certain industries can be exempt from government regulations and taxes *(Chapter 11)*.

The Code of Federal Regulations (CFR) consists of

50 volumes of procedures that all government employees and most industries are required to follow. Congress passes laws and the bureaucracy supposedly clari-
fies the laws into CFR defined controls. When you read
about certain corporations beating out the bureaucracy
and being exempted from the law, remember the secret
of their power is that they (or their lawyers) know the
difference between regulations and laws – they aren't
breaking the law, they are manipulating a regulation!

POINT TO PONDER

The information about volunteering is not new. Ayn Rand,
a noted philosopher and author, used much of her famous novel,
"Atlas Shrugged", to make similar points when government tricks
became obvious to her in the 1940's.

At one point in her book the scenario went like this as the
government tried to control the hero's special technique for making metal. The scene is a courtroom where a three judge panel
has summoned Hank Reardon. He has just been advised that
cases of this nature are not tried by a jury, but are tried by a three
judge panel appointed by the Bureau of Economic Planning and
National Resources. Reardon has just refused to enter a plea:

"Do you..." the judge stumbled; he had not expected it to
be that easy. "Do you throw yourself on the mercy of this court?"

"I do not recognize this court's right to try me."

"What?"

Hank Reardon repeated his statement.

"But, Mr. Reardon, this is the legally appointed court to try
this particular category of crime."

"I do not recognize my action as a crime."

"But you have admitted that you have broken our regulations controlling the sale of your metal."

"I do not recognize your right to control the sale of my
metal."

"Do you mean that you are refusing to obey the law?" asked
the judge.

"No. I am complying with the law — to the letter. Your law
holds that my life, my work and my property may be disposed of

without my consent. Very well, you may now dispose of me without my participation in the matter. I will not play the part of defending myself where no defense is possible, and I will not simulate the illusion of dealing with a tribunal of justice."

The dialogue in Ayn Rand's novel continues between Reardon and the court for another page and then the court questions if he is aware of the gravity of the charges against him and the sentence he could receive.

Reardon challenges the panel to impose their sentence.

"It is completely irregular," said the second judge. "The law requires you to submit a plea in your own defense. Your only alternative is to state for the record that you throw yourself on the mercy of the court."

"I do not."

"But you have to."

"Do you mean that what you expect from me is some sort of voluntary action?"

"Yes."

"I volunteer nothing."

"But the law demands that defendant's side be represented on the record."

"Do you mean that you need my help to make this procedure legal?"

"Well, no...yes...that is, to complete the form."

"I will not help you."

The exchange continues until the oldest judge smiles condoningly and says, "Mr. Reardon, it is regrettable that you should have misunderstood us so completely. That's the trouble — that businessmen refuse to approach us in a spirit of trust and friendship. They seem to imagine that we are their enemies. Why do you speak of human sacrifices? What made you go to such an extreme? We have no intention of seizing your property or destroying your life. We do not seek to harm your interests."

***

The insight Ayn Rand had in realizing what government was doing in the late 1940's and early 1950's is displayed in the books she wrote at that time. A better understanding of the attitudes which prevail among bureaucrats today, can be best developed by reading this great classic.— ATLAS SHRUGGED.

CHAPTER 4

VOLUNTEERING

Don't Volunteer for Nothin'

If you were directly asked to voluntarily give up your unalienable or Constitutional Rights, chances are you would reply with an emphatic "NO!" The truth is that you are being asked to surrender certain of your rights every day and you are doing it without even a murmur of complaint.

Did you take a driver's test before being issued a driver's license? Did you give the IRS information on your tax return which could be used against you in a court of law if you are accused of stretching the truth? Did you ever apply for a permit to add-on to your present house or a hunting license, or a permit to buy a fire-arm? Did you ever apply to a government agency for any permit to do something? Did you apply for a position with a company that requires you to submit any conflicts involving sexual harassment, discrimination or wages to binding arbitration?

Each time, you agreed to "voluntarily" surrender some of your rights!

You have the right to travel about freely in America without undue hindrance, harassment or restrictions by government, via the most common method of transportation within your means. Yet, you have allowed the government to usurp that right with a prior restraint rule. The rule is that you get a driver's license from a government agency. To do this you must prove, in advance, that you are qualified to exercise your rights as a citizen by taking certain tests. The test will supposedly permit a civil servant to determine if you are an unsafe driver. *(Chapter 15)*

A rule or regulation usually demands action on your part. The Constitution specifically forbids prior restraint and if possession of a driver's license was truly a mandatory law, it would do just that - prohibit you from driving until you proved yourself worthy. When you volunteered by applying for a driver's license, you agreed to give that rule, and any subsequent regulations, the force of law.

Ordinances or regulations, to be enforced as law, must have your explicit or implied agreement. Our constitutions (state and U.S.) do not make provisions for anyone to enact laws except the legislative branches of government. The Administrative Branch and the Judicial Branch can pass all the rrules and egulations they want regarding their own actions, but they have no authority to foist their regulations and procedures off as laws and then compel private citizens to obey them. They can, however, attempt to coerce, intimidate or bribe you to volunteer and accept their decrees as valid laws.

Sometimes the bribe is subtle and loaded with tricks. Sometimes it is obvious and reeks of Threats and Intimidation (T&I). You can go through ten kinds of hell fighting with an agency of government that is trying to enforce "voluntary" compliance with their rules. Their purpose is that you must be manipulated to volunteer or their bureaucracy will be without power. If they cannot exercise a power over you, then others may follow your lead and soon the bureaucrats will be out of a job.

One of the prerequisites the U.S. has for recognizing the validity of a foreign government is that the government in power must be "in control" of its citizens. That is the official position of our U.S. Department of State. If that is how our government feels about recognizing dictators, why should it hesitate to apply the same standards for our own bureaucracy? If the bureaucrat-controllers cannot keep you in line, they are out of work. Period! Now you know what motivates the control bureaucrats in their efforts to seduce and intimidate you to "voluntarily surrender your rights" and abide by their regulations.

In the private sector, more companies are requiring employees to submit to binding arbitration instead of filing a complaint with a court of law. Although it seems to be reasonable, keep in mind that the so-called impartial arbitrator (judge) does not have to follow rules of evidence and, since he or she charges upwards of several hundred dollars an hour, may be biased in favor of the company's position since that firm might use their arbitration services again – and it is unlikely that you will be a returning customer.

It is not easy to fight against the rules and still avoid being caught in the web of voluntary entrapment. It takes some thought and caution on your part. If you receive what appears to be an intimidating letter from the motor vehicle department, the city, the zoning board or any other agency of the government, do not take the "implied" threats literally. Do not make the mistake of initiating court action or negotiations. You may think the letter is threatening to violate your rights, but rest assured that it has been carefully worded to make you "believe", but unable to prove, such a threat has been made.

If you receive a certified letter or an official notice has been published notifying you that a "court" action has been instituted, then you must respond. You cannot ignore this! But your response can be as simple as a brief note stating: "I will not voluntarily permit anyone to usurp or minimize my rights, nor am I designating anyone to be a binding arbitrator in any disputes of rights or equity. If anyone has a constitutionally valid claim, they must follow the law according to the Constitution. I will remain an involuntary litigant in any such action and the claim is denied!"

When retaining counsel, always consider that lawyers are "officers of the court" and are required to adhere to the court's rules. Following normal court procedures can result in your being considered to have "volunteered for the rules" and subject you to the binding decisions of an arbitrator instead of a judge in a court of law.

The U.S. Supreme Court made a ruling in *Kelo v New London*, in 2005, in which the court stated that private property can be taken from one citizen for non-public use and given to another, as long as there would be a benefit to society. As a result the lawyers and media all concluded that the "taking" in urban renewal or "community development" programs was legal. To understand how the court could make such a ruling, we have to go back to *Square One*: Ms. Kelo started the court action when her rights weren't actually threatened. By starting litigation she "voluntarily" gave the question to the courts. *(Chapter 5)*

To avoid giving anyone the mistaken impression that you are submitting to or granting the court authority in any litigation, you or your attorney must preface any responses, remarks and appearances with the qualification that this is a "Special Appearance" or a "Special Response" to the action before the court. Some courts and even your own lawyer may attempt to panic you into making a voluntary plea or commitment.

Never initiate court action just because some official sounding agency appears to be threatening you. If the letter says "do this and comply with such and such within 10 days or appropriate legal action will be taken," you are probably the recipient of a meaningless threat. If you initiate an action with the courts to stop them from taking "appropriate legal action" you will lose! Normally, you cannot stop any government agency from doing its designated duty. Appropriate legal action is required of every government entity. If the implied threat is not "appropriate" (within the scope of governmental authority) then no lawful action can be taken. By initiating a fight in the courts, you will give the court authority to rule and since you are in court "voluntarily", the court's decision can be enforced.

The legal maxim "Volenti non fit injuria" can apply in all such cases. If you volunteer, you cannot claim injury as a result of your voluntary act. If you are not compelled into court via a summons (a real summons, not an Administrative Summons), you are volunteering and the court gets the entire question or case to rule on.

When you "voluntarily" enter into those stoic chambers known as the "Halls of Justice" you agree to abide by the procedures and rules of the court. Among those innumerable rules is one which permits the judge to rule for "public good" just as if the ruling was for "public use" or your individual Rights if you initiated the action. If you are in court voluntarily your interests can be considered secondary to those of society. You have agreed to abide by the court's decision

If you can think of something that the law "requires" you to do, you will find that it is a regulation or rule. If you are prohibited from doing something, most likely it is a valid law!

If you were in the Armed Forces, you might remember being advised early in boot camp "Don't Volunteer for Anything!" That was sage advice from your drill sergeant. From that time on, troops were often selected for undesirable or extremely dangerous duties by a process that included a "request" for volunteers - then an authoritative finger pointed at you and indicated you were "volunteering for duty." Didn't your drill instructor warn you not to volunteer? When that finger pointed your way and you obediently got up or stepped forward, you volunteered!

You can volunteer by serving on a committee and supposedly finding solutions to problems the community faces. Most of us feel honored when the government asks us for our opinion. But such commissions, boards, committees or panels are often nothing more than a subtle ruse to trick the public into going along with some government program that might otherwise encounter troublesome resistance. They also help shield the real culprits who are trying to get us to voluntarily surrender our rights. Blue-Ribbon panels shield the decision-maker more than they protect the public. Most government programs now require a "Citizen Advisory Committee" (or some similar sounding name) in order to protect corporate special interests and the bureaucrat controllers behind the scenes.

When you take any action, no matter how innocent it may appear, you are giving your consent and volunteering. Despite protection for accused criminals via the famous Miranda Decision, those rights do not apply to individuals when they have not been charged with an actual crime.

Under the *Miranda v. Arizona, 384 U.S. 436 (1966)* SCOTUS ruling, a criminal suspect cannot make a confession unless he has been forewarned of his rights and it is the responsibility of government to ascertain that the person is making the confession intelligently and voluntarily. On the civil side, when you are not charged with a crime and the government is trying to violate your rights by tricking you into volunteering, the courts will take the opposite tack and permit the government to coerce you into volunteering without a warning or advising you of your legal rights.

If you owned property along a river bank and the water was constantly eroding your shore and carrying away your property, what would you do?

The Environmental Protection Agency (EPA) regulations and procedures emphatically imply you can do nothing without first getting EPA approval. The moment you apply for "permission" to put some rocks along your bank to stop the erosion, you open a

Pandora's Box that could result in the complete loss of your property.

Remember: When you ask for permission, you imply that the agency has authority and you volunteer to go along with their rules. One of their regulations is that you must submit a plan, complete with an environmental impact study. That study could cost you thousands of dollars in engineering and research fees and take several months to complete. By the time EPA gives its approval, half of your land could be down-stream and the cost of the impact reports greater than the value of the remaining property.

If you just "do it" without asking permission, what can the EPA do? Chances are they will not do a thing except demand explanations or that forms be filled out. Filling out such forms could again subject you to the jurisdiction of the EPA rules and regulations. The EPA, if it has the budget and was so disposed, might conduct its own environmental impact study on your little project, at government expense. If they felt they could actually prove you did some specific damage to the environment, they could file a lawsuit (Due Process) and get a court order to have you restore the area to its pre-project condition. The possibilities of this happening are virtually zilch and zero.

Don't ask for permission - they may say no! It is your property and you have a right to take any reasonable action to protect it. Do not let any power seeker convince you otherwise.

When you find yourself subjected to adjudication by a commissioner or arbitrator (even those calling themselves "judge"), rather than by a real judge in a real court of law, you are being exposed to legal trickery called Principled Adjudication — a theory the U.S. Supreme Court approves of and follows, allowing a designated officer of the court to make decisions based on the principles of *Stare Decisis*. Usually such kangaroo tribunals can be avoided if you are tenacious and demand a trial by a qualified court of competent jurisdiction. Principled adjudication is the legal system's method of providing buffers for the judges.

LEGAL DEFINITIONS

VOLUNTARILY—Done by design or intention, intentional, proposed or not accidental. Intentionally and without coercion. Young v. Young, 148 Kan. 876, 84 P.2d 916, 917.

VOLUNTARY—Unimpelled by another's influence; spontaneous; acting of oneself. Coker v. State, 199 Ga. 20, 33 S.E. 2d 171, 174.

VOLUNTARY JURISDICTION—In old English law, a jurisdiction exercised by certain courts in matters were there is no opposition. 3 Bl. Comm. 66.

WILLFUL - Proceeding from a conscious motion of the will; intending the result which actually comes to pass; designed; intentional ; malicious. *(More in Chapter 26)*

CHAPTER 5

SCOTUS BUFFERS
Traps Waiting To Ensnare You

Every year the Supreme Court of The United States receives over 4,000 legal petitions from private citizens and corporations for review of some case or law that is considered in conflict with the U.S. Constitution. SCOTUS can accept or reject any such petitions (writs of certiorari) "without comment". When they do so, they mislead the public, the media, legislators, lower courts and attorneys. Many assume the law or rulings of lower courts were "valid" - when, in fact, SCOTUS just decided they didn't want to be bothered. If SCOTUS was required to clearly and specifically state its reasons for refusing to grant a review, each time one was requested, there would be a better understanding of our laws, a better system of justice and greater respect for the laws and our Constitution. The Supreme Court usually has previous decisions and legal maxims which they use as a basis for denying review, but they rarely tell the litigants or their attorneys what they are - even if they were made 50, 75 or 150 years ago! If The Supreme Court Of The United States was really concerned with "justice for all," it would never permit misleading rulings to take effect!

Courts and officers of the court (lawyers) are expected

to follow the common law maxim of *"Stare Decisis Et Non Quieta Movere"* - That means "let the decision stand and do not disturb things which have been settled." It could also be construed to mean "We've made up our collective minds, played the trick and we do not want to be confused with more facts."

Most courts are gutless when they refuse to hear arguments of law as well as variations of facts. They fall back on precedent to avoid making a decision that could upset their own little world. Dispensing justice is often ignored as a purpose of the courts if it means going against the principle of "stare decisis." Such a legal maxim can be used to coerce otherwise honest and competent judges into going along with procedures that are contrary to the laws, individual rights and the Constitution.

The Supreme Court of The United States (SCOTUS) considers that it has the duty to try and uphold any legislation passed. To do this the nine-members often agree to accept questions that will allow a distorted but favorable ruling for the government. Such was the case when the courts wanted to stop getting the question of "taking" property for private use in urban renewal or community development cases, such as *Kelo v. City of New London,545 U.S 469 (2005).*

The plaintiff in that case was Susette Kelo who did not want to sell her house to a private developer who had grandiose plans for a community development. Ms Kelo made the mistake of hiring an attorney to institute court action to stop what she assumed to be a "threat" to condemn her property. After objecting to efforts to buy her property, she found an official notice on her door that she could either sell her property to the developer or have it condemned. What she and her attorney did not realize is that the "condemnation" referred to in the notice would be *"inverse condemnation." (See Chapter 6)*

Because of the vast number of properties involved, residential, business, government and industrial, SCOTUS accepted the question because the litigant was not forced into the court system and subsequently ruled that government can "take" property (or force the sale) for "public good." That ruling, misleading as it was, is now used as a buffer to discourage lawyers from submitting the question to the courts again – Stare Decisis!

When the Obama Administration went to SCOTUS regarding the Affordable Care Act (ACA or Obamacare) with a question about "mandatory" participation, the high court legislated from the bench and changed the meaning of the word "penalty" to "tax" in order to justify the law.

If you or your lawyer start an action in the courts, you are voluntarily giving the court authority to act as a binding arbitrator and you are agreeing to abide by the rules of the court. The rules of the court (which lawyers, as officers of the court are required to abide by) are that when a litigant's Constitutional Rights are not violated, the court may rule for public good. If you volunteer to go into court or you do not challenge the court authority, you are considered to have volunteered and therefore your rights cannot be violated by a ruling for public good rather than your individual rights!

Government bureaucrats are not going to meet you head on. They invariably try to have buffers in the game to take the brunt of your criticisms and retaliations when you discover that they are using trickery to manipulate you, limit your rights or take your property.

The Miranda decision orders that an accused criminal must be informed of his rights. The Supreme Court ruled "...a valid waiver will not be presumed simply from the silence of the accused...." Can't we, the non-criminals, be given similar consideration by the courts?

The Courts say we cannot! That is their ruling. If you voluntarily give the court jurisdiction, you will lose. Unless your lawyer is on his toes, he may inadvertently volunteer you to follow the bureaucratic rule process or enter into the twisted justice system almost every time you consult him or her. You must pay close attention to every word and phrase uttered by a bureaucrat or court or you may find yourself volunteering to become a slave to government.

TEST YOURSELF:

Will the courts force you to sell your property, involuntarily, to a private entity or person for their own personal use or development?

Can the courts legally order you to sell or transfer your property to another for their private use or development?

The correct answer to the first question is "NO." The answer to the second is "YES." The questions are similar but different. It is the manner in which a question is phrased that will allow you to determine the differences between rules and laws. The Courts cannot order you to sell or transfer your property to another for private use unless: enforcing a contract; you failed to pay your mortgage or a real lien; if you had agreed to sell the property and then tried to back out, the court could order you to either pay the damages or surrender title; or if you have "voluntarily" submitted the question to the court!

Another procedure SCOTUS endorses is that of the "non-published" ruling of a court. This is used when a court hears a matter and feels compelled to rule contrary to popular control procedures. To avoid having the ruling cited in subsequent cases, the ruling goes out as a "non-published" finding.

A challenge to a California law regarding drivers' licenses was eventually granted, but rather than have everyone know that the DL was not required, the court made a non-published ruling. If you want to see it, you will have to know the name of the attorney who filed it and won.

The exposure of the tricks require checking out the early process and reading the documentation. Usually you can find the basis for a misleading ruling early in the proceedings.

It would be a life's work for one author to check every detail of SCOTUS and lower court rulings. Often the rulings come as a result of how the question is presented to the courts. If you were to ask, "Do I have to do whatever the government says?" Most likely the answer would be "No!" But if your lawyer phrases the question for the court as, "Can government require me to do what it says?" you have left the door open for the court to rule on time, place, circumstance and definitions of words like "require". The answer will most likely be construed to mean "Yes!"

The *"Citizens United v FEC"* ruling from SCOTUS

declared that corporations, like citizens, can spend money on political campaigns as a matter of "free speech." That ruling now allows foreign countries like China, Iran, Russia, Pakistan and others to sway our elections - and the donors aren't even identified.

When The Supreme Court of the United States ruled that corporations have First Amendment free speech rights, the same as individual citizens, they screwed the American people! That ruling by SCOTUS opened the door for corporations, owned and controlled by foreign governments, to sway our election and legislative processes.

Corporations are not people! These entities exist because some state government says they exist – and they are nothing more than a bureaucratic extension of government. Wherever created, corporations are not allowed to do business in every state without first registering their corporate papers with each state. They apply to register as "foreign corporations" doing business in the state and their applications (subject to denial) include the legal purposes of the corporation and agreement that it will operate "within the scope of all laws and regulations". No state government will allow a foreign corporation to violate the state's laws or regulations. Corporations are not people – they exist because some state (not the federal government) says they exist.

As the SCOTUS ruling is being applied, several Chinese corporations can own stock in an American-based XYZ corporation registered in Delaware. That Delaware corporation is then entitled, as a matter of free speech, to donate large sums of money to a SuperPac that will then place advertising designed to support or defeat issues (virtual candidates) that would be of benefit to China rather than the citizens of the U.S.A. Although the SuperPacs are not permitted to communicate or consult with a candidate's campaign, they are allowed to run advertising that would seriously impact various candidates, their campaigns, voter issues and the actual election process!

If The Supreme Court Of The United States was really concerned with "justice for all," it would never permit misleading rulings to take effect! When the Court rules, the media and the legal profession then assist the courts in continuing their trickery to avoid upholding the Constitutionally protected Rights of the people.

> *". . . corporations have no consciences, no beliefs, no feelings, no thoughts, no desires. Corporations help structure and facilitate the activities of human beings, to be sure, and their 'personhood' often serves as a useful legal fiction. But they are not themselves members of "We the People" by whom and for whom our Constitution was established."*
> *~Supreme Ct Justice Stevens, Jan. 2010*

CHAPTER 6

HUD TRICKS
TO TAKE YOUR PROPERTY

Keep in mind that the legal experts are extremely efficient in changing the words and terms that describe their tricks. Nothing really changes except the words and procedures – the smoke and mirror tricks continue to exist.

There are 5 volumes of CFR manuals dedicated just to Housing and Urban Development (HUD) rules and regulations. The CFR rules used by HUD (Title 24) are more extensive than those of any other agency except for the Department of Agriculture (USDA) and the IRS. These regulations outline procedures the promoters and various government agencies must follow. It can guide them every step of the way in "legally" taking a person's rights and property from them.

The promoter who wants possession of a certain property or home may have been approached by local government instead of the other way around. Sometimes local officials want to enhance their tax base for property they feel could be better utilized for something other than the old homes or businesses that have occupied the land and paid taxes for years. If it is a major city, chances are the local government already has a department and staff completely familiar with the HUD programs and procedures. In a small town the promoter might have to take a staff member or the mayor by the hand and lead them through the procedures outlined by HUD for deceitful but legalized property confiscation.

Whether the city announces it wants a Neighborhood Development project and seeks a developer or the promoter-developer approaches the local government, the end result is usually the same: A special government employee is appointed to work with the local government and developer in acquiring the land and financing needed for the project.

Usually the area is researched and then designated a "Target Area." This description can have devastating effects on a community and the people who do business or live there. Such a designation causes mortgage lenders and banks to shy away from any dealings with it. Property owners who are thinking of developing or improving their own premises find they are prevented from doing so by inability to find suitable financing, opposition from zoning and building boards, and reluctance on the part of all bureaucrats to be directly involved in any disputes. Permission to do just about anything is denied and if the owner wants to sell and get paid immediately, he finds the promoter isn't ready to buy yet and other potential buyers are reluctant to make an offer since they think they would not be able to use the property the way they would like.

If ever a person felt like the victim of an attacking enemy force, this would be it! The government, instead of operating in a manner to protect your individual and property rights, is actually preventing you from full enjoyment and use of your real estate. The property owners begin to feel that being in a Target Area means they are going to be "bombed out" any day.

Because of all this, the property values in the area are depressed and this is used as justification to re-designate it as a "blighted area" and appoint a committee of citizens to study and suggests ways to improve the community. The citizens group becomes the buffer!

Special government employees enter the picture and, along with local bureaucrats, they "guide" the committee into accepting and adopting a project that would revitalize and enhance the area. Some of the citizens display the typical human trait of greed when they can see that if the project goes in, the property they own across the street might quadruple in value. They are quick to agree to any such shopping center or complex the city might suggest. They ignore the fact that their neighbors might be tricked into losing or selling their family homes for a mere pittance.

The CFR manuals for HUD are insistent that no project can be instituted unless there is a Citizens' Advisory board or committee. This is HUD's way of shifting the blame if anyone says HUD is being dictatorial and abusive of its agency. They simply blame the Official Citizen's Advisory Committee. Always keep in mind that all the regulations in the CFR manuals hold that any action by a citizen, either by making application or appealing a decision, gives credence to the authority and validity of the previous actions taken by that agency.

The Rules of HUD, the laws of Congress and the limitations of the U.S. Constitution prohibit the "forceful" taking of property for Public Good, so there could be no "implied threat." When your lawyer files to restrain the government from doing something it was already prohibited from doing, the lawyer springs the trap, ensnares his clients in the tangled web and makes the court a binding arbitrator. When the clients allow their lawyer (an officer of the court) to file such an action, they have agreed to abide by the findings of the court. Under those rules, when a party is in court voluntarily, the court can rule for what the judge perceives to be the "public good", rather than your individual rights. Such decisions can be appealed, but that puts the entire burden, evidentiary and financial, on you as the appellant.

If the city had been planning to build a public park, a highway or street, they could rightfully use Eminent Domain and have the property condemned for public use. This would be a legal action. The only matter that could properly be argued would be the price to be paid. The property would be for public use! There are even limitations on the eminent domain procedure, such as the government having to prove a real need for the project with no viable alternatives.

A lower court might refuse to be tricked into applying such deceitful rules to take someone's home or property and decide in their favor - especially if the people still elect the judges. But the previously referenced rule of "Stare Decisis" is at work and the developer and city could easily appeal the matter. Eventually the HUD position would be upheld by a higher court and the couple would be forced to sell their home for the public good because they had volunteered. And just to make certain this would be the outcome (so the lawyers can be buffers to discourage their clients from filing such actions) SCOTUS accepted and ruled in the previously mentioned *Kelo v New London* case. But the justices did warn that anyone applying this process must do so carefully – ie: trick the litigants into volunteering.

It is the legal maxim - Volenti Non Fit Injuria — If someone volunteers, they cannot claim injury. The courts have many rules that are designed to confound not only the average citizen, but cause many lawyers to walk out of the court room scratching their heads in amazement. They do not understand what really happened or why they lost the battle!

The secret of real power to protect your property is to "do nothing" — the hardest thing of all! Let the developer or city actually file a legal action in the courts (they have no grounds) and then challenge the basis for the suit and the jurisdiction of the court. Make no motions that could grant any validity to the claim. Preface all responses and appearances with that all important qualifier word, "SPECIAL", and make sure that it includes the statement that you are not volunteering for public good or acknowledging jurisdiction or compelling government interests. Any legal papers served on you or your attorney must be actual "Court Orders" signed by a real judge – not an administrative judge (commissioner or arbitrator).

Don't get cutesy in dealing with these people and think you can hold out for the top dollar while all those around you are being tricked into selling. Plans for a commercial development can be altered to include a little public park for public use, where your property is located. That would be a different fight. Get the picture? Your best protection is in being united with your neigh-

bors. Let everyone know how to resist the land grab-
bers. Courts do not have jurisdiction over you and your
property except as provided for in the Constitution or if
you voluntarily grant jurisdiction. Eminent domain can
only be used for "public use" (parks, streets, highways,
etc.).

Remember—If you think something is not fair, there
is a good possibility that you are Right!

If you challenge the people who want to take your
property or that of your neighbors, you will often be
told that "you don't understand the situation." Don't
believe it! The Constitution has not been changed regarding eminent domain (despite SCOTUS double-
speak in the Kelo v New London case) — it still reads;
in part, in the Fifth Amendment: "No person shall
be...deprived of life, liberty or property without due
process of law; nor shall private property be taken for
public use, without just compensation."

Obviously, if it cannot be taken for public use without "just" compensation and due process, it certainly
cannot be taken for private use or public good under
any such circumstances – unless you volunteer! Due
process is often whatever the courts say it is, but it does
mean following the laws — not just the rules of the
court. Unless the land is being taken for actual public
use, it cannot be taken unless you previously volunteered and consented to abide by the rulings of the
courts.

You can use some laws to protect yourself, your Rights
and your property. Anyone who conspires with another
to violate your rights, by trickery, or fraud, may be subject to criminal and civil liability under existing Fed-

eral and State Racketeering Laws (RICO).

When a Target Area development was being planned for one community and after several years and millions of dollars was spent by HUD, I sent a letter to property owners who had attended a meeting called by a Citizens Advisory Committee. It explained how the trick was being played and was enough to make the city and HUD officials reconsider their position.

After restating the information verbally at a meeting, a spokesman for the HUD project immediately challenged the advice I had given the audience. He suggested that since I was not a lawyer, the people should go to an attorney and then "have their day in court" or "request condemnation proceedings."

You already know about the "day in court" trick. Requesting condemnation is something else!

REQUESTING CONDEMNATION

You can "request" that condemnation proceedings be initiated by the city. You cannot be forced into it for such a purpose, but you can request (volunteer) for it. Of course, there are some tax advantages in having your property condemned. The technical name is *"Inverse Condemnation"* — your lawyer should be able to tell you what it means and how it works, but you still have to volunteer for it.

A few weeks after the confrontation and notice, the daily newspapers printed several articles about how the developer was dropping out "because no contract was offered" and he could not raise needed financing. With all the tax free bond issues and government secured loans available, at very low interest rates, this was really a pitiful excuse used for public consumption to avoid having everyone realize why the project was being killed. A few more weeks passed and the city announced the project was put on hold - after five years and $5 Million was spent. A month later a few businessmen were encouraged to petition the city to abandon the plans and permit them to get on with their individual development of their own properties. The city and HUD reluctantly complied! They saved face and could continue with their legal theft programs in other areas where the people were not so well informed.

If someone approaches you to see if you are willing to sell and you suspect it may be a ploy of a HUD endorsed project, you must qualify any discussion with "I am not opening negotiations with you at this time. If you or your clients want to submit an offer to buy my property, I might take it into consideration. But this shall not be construed as a solicitation of an offer or an opening of any form of negotiations."

It may sound cumbersome, but without it, even a discussion could be construed as "opening negotiations." According to HUD's CFR rules, if you open negotiations, after six months they can claim to have a legal cause of action to take you to court and get a valid court order to force you to sell your property or pay damages.

MORE TRICKS OF THE PAST

When the State of Arizona decided it wanted more control over every aspect of life in that state the bureaucrats formed a Water Management Control Agency and filed a real lawsuit against every property owner in the state. Water rights went with every deed. To further their cause they sent out notices to every property owner, via Certified Mail, that each was named in the pending lawsuit. At the same time the various water companies around the state notified their customers that the water company would "protect their rights" and they would not have to answer the lawsuit. The result was a quiet, voluntary default judgment against the water owners (property owners) with control of water passing to the government bureaucrats. When strictly enforced this program allows the water-crats complete control over most property unless the owner can find a way to "personally" drill a well or use the land without water or waste. In this case the court was used as the buffer. Subsequent court decisions will use the legal maxim of Stare Decisis to continue with this abuse of private property and the legal system.

In Monroe County, Florida, made up of hundreds of small and medium sized tropical islands or keys (Florida Keys), the state bureaucrats technically ordered the county to stop issuing building permits to anyone until it complied with a Federal Housing & Urban Development (HUD) master-plan program. The HUD plan is to trick every city and county in the nation to submit Master Plans for their area. Those Master Plans are then construed to be a voluntary commitment on the part of local government. Local officials are then told by state officials (the buffers) that they must do certain things to comply with the Master Plan.

When Monroe County officials heard that they were supposed to cease issuing building permits, they sent a formal question to the state and HUD officials. The letter asked "Is it true that we are ordered to stop issuing building permits as of July 1st?" That is the interpretation the local officials had placed on the information they received. The State of Florida did not reply. HUD officials did not answer the question. The County had asked the question wrong — or right — depending on your point of view. If they had merely asked, "Is it true that we are not supposed to issue any more building permits after July 1st?" the State and HUD would have promptly responded "Yes!"

The state and HUD did not have authority to "order" Monroe County to violate the rights of its citizens by denying them permits to build on their property. Such a procedure might collapse the theory that any government agency has any real authority to dictate what a person may do with his own private property. As long as the property is not utilized in direct violation of deed restrictions or zoning rules existing at the time of purchase, they can, within reason, do anything they want. If the government or a neighbor believes the use is detrimental to the property rights of others, then they have the burden of proof to take the matter to a court of competent jurisdiction and prove the damages.

If the county refused to issue building permits, which most people believe they are required to have, the county officials are acting innocently. The county believes it is under orders from higher up and becomes the buffer between the property owners and the state, while the state is the buffer between the county and HUD to enforce the HUD rules.

Similar tactics are used to enforce the "Wetlands Act" and to take private property rights via the creation of so-called Marine Sanctuaries and no-fishing areas.

Big Brother bureaucrats appear to prefer introducing

their twisted programs in fast growing areas such as Florida, Arizona, Nevada, Southern Texas and Southern California. One disgruntled government employee said it was because the people don't have as many "old roots" and political contacts in those states. They are less likely to have a close relative in a position of authority within local government and less likely to be inclined to organize a group to fight and resist efforts to limit their rights.

The Florida Keys came under another scurrilous attack by Federal and State government when they attempted to use the same type of tricks used in HUD takeovers. Officially the entire area was declared a "Marine Sanctuary" and a citizen's group was appointed to determine the methods that would be employed to carry out the protection of the "sanctuary." This is now being used to help major hotel corporations take-over more valuable lands to build more hotels; make commercial lobster trapping too expensive and thereby open the door to foreign interests to ship "farmed lobster" into the U.S. without resistance or competition.

Similar commissions and agencies are wreaking havoc on the fishing and lobster industry in the New England states and the influence of foreign companies that "farm" competitive fish is being felt by generations of Americans. Those foreign fish farmers can donate funds to political action committees and put American fishermen out of business - thanks to the SCOTUS ruling in Citizens United.

Do Not Surrender!
When you challenge the rules you weaken those
rules and that will strengthen the real laws!

CHAPTER 7

BLACK OPS
Big Business Is Using the Rules

Just signing a petition for some great program or idea isn't enough. If the movement is really important, you have to check out "who" is really behind the effort. Are they working at this to accomplish what the petition states or are they part of a "Black Ops" effort used by major organizations - the Judas Goat technique?

Let us assume there seems to be public support for the repeal of a law or regulation. Your firm benefits from that law and you do not want it repealed, but you don't want to take an unfavorable public relations position of being in favor of it, either. What do you do?

Using the black ops strategy, from behind the scenes you can financially support and start a committee with a stated purpose to "Repeal the Law." Make lots of noise for the media about how the group is going to get signatures on petitions to bring the law to a vote of the people. Hire a chairman and recruit several nice looking old ladies (volunteers) to set up tables at local shopping centers so there will be sufficient exposure to make it appear that the petition drive is underway. In most states it is illegal to get people to sign a petition and then throw the petition away, so you make sure they do not get too many signatures. You only want to manipulate the system – not break the law!

Move some ladies and their card tables to the shopping malls around the city or state and send out occasional press releases about how well the petition drive is proceeding. Then, about a week before the filing deadline, you can plant a negative story about lack of support and volunteers - but don't tell anyone where to go if they actually want to volunteer to get petitions signed.

Finally, a day or two before the filing deadline to put the issue on the ballot, let the public know that the committee will probably be short of the required number of signatures. The deadline comes and there are not enough valid signatures. If the Black Ops manipulators feel really brave, they submit the petitions and have someone carefully verify the authenticity. Even though they have just enough signatures, there are always many signers who are not registered or otherwise not legally qualified to sign petitions. They could further hedge their efforts by making sure that one of the little old ladies is "not-registered" to vote and that could disqualify all the signatures she collects. The issue never gets on the ballot and the company can continue to profit from the unpopular law.

Check The Leaders And Followers

Is there a Black Ops person in charge? The old saying "Follow the money!" is what must be applied when determining who is behind a movement. Just accepting someone at face value is not sufficient if you want your efforts to be effective. You must know something of that person's background, former employers, activities and their personal source of revenue. If the organization has lots of funding (more than the pitiful donations normally received from the members or public) it is important that you know the source. It could be from some company or individual who is conducting deep cover black-ops that are contrary to what you want to accomplish. Not only does it work against you, it results in you believing that your efforts are worthwhile and takes you away from a more practical use of your money, talents and efforts on some other campaign.

The highly regulated industries in many states have lobbyists pushing for rules they can use. When the liquor-wholesalers in one state did not want to sell booze and supplies to bars on credit, they asked to have a law passed that prohibited the sale of alcoholic beverages on credit. The public and bar owners assumed this meant they could no longer run a long tab for their customers. The saloon keepers did not complain since it would probably save them a few bucks in the long run. Eventually, the liquor control people pulled out the sleeper and ordered the wholesalers to stop selling to the bars and liquor stores on credit. When the delivery was made, the retailers had to pay up front for the liquor – no credit! The wholesaler innocently stated "It's the law!"

Insurance firms are great at getting regs passed for their own benefit *(See Chapter 12)*. How about protecting incompetent mechanics from being viewed by the car owner? Just get OSHA to pass a rule that prohibits the public from entering the work area, and then blame it on the insurance company that requires the insured business to abide by OSHA regulations. If you have the clout, you can get a government regulating agency to pass such a regulation and then blame it on the "law."

My first awareness of being able to profit from the passage of an unpopular law came when I was only 10 years old. We lived in Wichita, Kansas, and the state was dry — hard alcohol was illegal and my father was a bootlegger. One day my father took me into town and told me to wait in the car when he parked in front of the Baptist church. My father was never religious and I was curious. We always attended Catholic church but he would not go along. When he came out, I asked why he went to a Baptist church.

"I gave a contribution to the church fund to keep whiskey illegal in Kansas," he explained. The money, he said, came from several small bootleggers in the area. He pointed out that, "If the law is changed to make the sale of whiskey legal, I'll be out of business. So, we want to keep the law and so does the Baptist church."

Whether you choose to abide by a regulation, break a rule or have an ordinance passed and enforced for your benefit, you must always remember that volunteering will give it all the force and effect of a valid law. You can be fined, subjected to exceptional legal harassment and even go to jail for breaking such a regulation or rule.

You cannot always depend on your lawyer to help you. Many of the tricky court procedures, rules and regulations being enforced as law today were put into effect in the 1950's and 60's. Few, if any, lawyers practicing today were even in born in the 50's. Attorneys who know the variables between rules, regulations and laws usually discover it on their own. The law schools do not do an effective job of teaching them the subtle differences.

If you pick up any copy of the numerous volumes

entitled the Code of Federal Regulations (CFR), the rules by which the Federal bureaucracy is required to operate, you would believe you are reading actual laws. Lawyers are exposed to the CFR in law school and since the manuals read like law books, it is difficult to blame them if they do not always recognize the difference.

Usually your lawyer will try to keep you within the confines of the rules and regulations as well as the laws. It is easier for him to advise you and he may not even be aware of the dissimilarity. If you are lucky enough to have an attorney who is still willing to learn (that means he or she keeps their ego in check), you will be way ahead by giving that lawyer this book. If, as is often the case, your lawyer tries to double-talk you with the mysticisms of the legal system and lets that influential lawyer-ego get in the way of learning more about the legal system from a lay-person, then you would be well advised to seek other counsel.

Since you cannot have contact with your lawyer every minute of every day just to answer your question "Is it a law or a regulation?" you will have to keep certain things in mind, especially when you deal with government employees (police or clerks). Most do not know the differences and will often resist your efforts to explain it to them.

LAWS are written in such a manner as to prohibit an action that would violate the rights of another. You are prohibited by law from stealing your neighbor's car. You are prohibited from hitting your neighbor in the nose or taking such other violent actions as to disturb the peace and tranquility of others. You are prohibited from trespassing on the private property of others. You are prohibited from violating the Rights of others. With this as the purpose, such are our laws. Valid laws are for everyone - there are no licenses to violate a law!

REGULATIONS AND RULES are written in such a manner as to regulate our activity and behavior. Usually, a regulation will order you to do something which, if mandatory, would exceed the limited Constitutional authority of government and violate your Unalienable Rights in the process. These rules are supposed to keep us peacefully happy and content to follow the orders of our government superiors. Since rules and regulations are voluntary in nature, the rule-making authority can make and license exceptions!

YOU CAN BEAT THEM!

A DIFFERENT DRUMMER

In the late 1950's and early 1960's when HUD was first involved with unpopular Urban Renewal Projects, there was a rule prohibiting HUD from putting money into a project if a city did not have a federally approved Housing Code.

Building Codes and Housing Codes are different. The Building Code states the manner in which a new house or structure will be erected, size of electrical wiring, type of water lines, etc. It is the code professional contractors agree to follow when they construct a house. It is often applied to anyone who makes application for a remodeling permit and they are then required (as a condition of the un-required permit) to bring the entire structure up to the building code standards.

A Housing Code, on the other hand, attempts to tell the home owner that he must make certain changes in his structure, plumbing, wiring, etc., when he is not making any changes or even applying for a permit. The housing codes are often used by city inspectors to imply authority to come into a home and make sure it is up to the latest standards of the building code.

Citizens in a major U.S. city objected to the Housing Code and repealed it. The city council was upset since they thought that they could not qualify for certain Federal funding. They offered the Housing Code back to the people with some changes. The people voted "no" again. Eventually HUD changed its rules so that cities did not have to have a Housing Code to qualify for the Federal funds.

The Word Is ... NOT INalienable, when referring to our UNALIENABLE RIGHTS!

Our founding fathers signed the Declaration of Independence and confirmed the existence of our "...unalienable Right to life, liberty and the pursuit of happiness."

Over the years the dictionaries have been gradually abridged to put more emphasis on the word INalienable than the word UNalienable. UN- is an English prefix meaning "not" and is never qualified. The prefix IN- is Latin and also means "not" but is almost always qualified.

The prefix "in-" is often used in legal matters (inadmissible instead of not admissible) with the word being qualified – not at this time or place or under these circumstances.

If we allow continued misapplication of these words, we will soon find that our "Unalienable" Rights will be considered "Inalienable" and the courts will rule that the commonly accepted prefix will mean our Rights do not apply at this time, in this place or under these circumstances. This is just one final way we will lose our Unalienable Rights!

CHAPTER 8

WORD ABUSE
Distorted Language

The best defense you can develop against the usurping of your rights is to stay informed of current news and activity. Most men always manage to find a few minutes to read about sports and women seldom miss the advice to the lovelorn. The Internet and smart-phone Apps get a work-out as users search for specific information or news. Don't stop! All reading is informative, but do not limit what you read to a few favorite subjects. The sports scores, who will not play in Sunday's game and your favorite humorist will not save your home from a greedy developer.

Changing the publicly and legally accepted meanings of words is an on-going technique employed by the courts and the controllers. This results in changing our entire government system without amending the Constitution. If the founding fathers had included a reference to a dictionary that defined the words as they intended this trick could not be played on the people. But they didn't do that so the people have to be on their toes to stop the constant attempts to subvert the checks and balances drafted into our Constitution.

We all think we know the meaning of certain words and a fairly common word in use is "privilege." That word refers to something that is granted or given by one of authority to another individual and can be taken away by that authority. There is a constant movement by the judiciary, legislature and even major corporations to inter-change the accepted meaning of various terms. A good example of this is when Supreme Court justices use the word "privilege" in place of the word "Right" (as in Unalienable Right). It doesn't happen just once in a while – it is a constant abuse of the language with the end result being a gradual change in the legal and publicly accepted meaning of the words. SCOTUS has made a number of rulings in which the high court justices referred to the Fifth Amendment as a "privilege" rather than a Right reserved to the people. If public perception accepts it is a privilege it can eventually be rescinded by the authorities.

Bill Cosby, once one of TV's top entertainers and an expert in education, suggested that people could absorb much more news and information about current events if they would skim newspaper and magazine articles. The same applies to other information devices when you can type in a search for specific words. The procedure is to make a list of key words and when you are skimming, let those words be like flashing red lights to stop your eyes from scanning and focus on the subject matter. Those key words will let you know which articles to read slowly and carefully.

Bureaucrat controllers are quite adept at playing on words. It has been helping them to garner more and more power and control over you and your family. They manipulate words and have even slipped legislation past lawmakers by merely mis-naming the proposed bill before the legislature.

To make it easy for bureaucrat-controllers to circumvent the U.S. Constitution and your Rights, without actually violating the Constitution, the U.S. Supreme Court has come up with some changes in the definition of certain words. The Justices may not have done this to intentionally weaken the nation, even though that is the result. Their motivations were to uphold the acts of Congress. In some instances, Congress passes bills that directly conflict with the intentions of the Constitution. To avoid this, such words as "required", "must", "shall" and "may", have been given interchangeable definitions. In doing this the Supreme Court has caused almost all laws or regulations to be unconstitutionally vague.

Here are the definitions from Black's Law Dictionary:

MAY—An auxiliary verb qualifying the meaning of another verb by expressing ability, competency, liberty, permission, possibility, probability or contingency.

SHALL—As used in statutes, contracts, or the like, this word is generally imperative or mandatory. It has the invariable significance of excluding the idea of discretion, and has the significance of operating to impose a duty which may be enforced, particularly if public policy is in favor of this meaning, or when addressed to public officials, or where a public interest is involved, or where the public or persons have rights which ought to be exercised or enforced, unless a contrary intention appears. But it may be construed as merely permissive or directory (as equivalent to "may"), to carry out the legislative intention and in cases where no right or benefit to anyone depends on it being taken in the imperative sense, and where no public or private right is impaired by its interpretation in the other sense.

MUST—This word, like the word "shall" is primarily of mandatory effect and in that sense is used in antithesis to "may." But this meaning of the word is not the only one, and it is often used in a merely directory sense, and consequently is a synonym for the word "may" not only in the permissive sense of that word but also in the mandatory sense which it sometimes has.

REQUIRE—To direct, order, demand, instruct, command, claim, compel, request, need, exact. To be in need of. To ask for authoritatively or imperatively.
***

If you cannot adjust each and every one of these legal definitions to suit your desire, you should take a course in English language. Every law, regulation and ordinance in existence uses one or more of these words and the variable definitions leave it up to the reader or the court to decide which meaning to apply. In effect, SCOTUS has ruled that such words be given mandatory construction unless such an application violates someone's rights - then it is given a "voluntary construction." That means if your rights would be violated by the mandatory definition, you must be tricked or coerced into volunteering so the regulation can have the force of a mandatory law without violating your rights. This play on vague word definitions keeps lawyers and others in business or employed. It also chips away at your Unalienable Rights.

The biggest private sector of users or abusers of these

rules and regulations are hospitals, insurance companies, banks and major hotel and property developers. Anyone who wants to use such rules can go on-line and down-load a copy of the CFR manuals for HUD (or buy a hard copy) and find a way to secure all kinds of funding and methods to legally steal their neighbor's property. Within those pages you will find all the regulations you need to carry out a project. If, on the other hand, you do not want some developer taking your house, "Do Nothing" unless an actual lawsuit is filed in a court of competent jurisdiction! That is the secret of power over all the regulations and rules. They cannot use their rules to force you out of your property unless you volunteer!

More Abuse of Words

Prior to the passage of the Privacy Act of 1974, it was virtually impossible for anyone to get information about your personal income tax return. The IRS jealously guarded that information. But the so-called Privacy Act opened the door so that almost any government agency could have access to your financial information. Even foreign governments can get the data on your IRS tax return. Was that really a Privacy Act? Or was it a Non-Privacy Act? Do our Congressmen know what they did? Have they taken any action to correct this blight on the privacy of citizens?

The IRS Directors are often quoted as they call our income tax system "Voluntary." The payment of "acknowledged taxes" may be mandatory, but the reporting system is definitely voluntary. The IRS rule writers have become extremely efficient in trying to phrase every word and form to make you think you are required to file without saying that you are "required" to file a tax return *(See Chapter 26)*. Keep in mind when any agency says they "require this information" that the word require also means "need" or "ask for".

Those who utilize this knowledge and refuse to file a 1040 form or any other kind of tax return were often referred to by the Internal Revenue Service as "Illegal Tax Protesters." It was a neat play on words, but left the question: "Are they protesters of an illegal tax, or are they illegal protesters of the tax?" Current IRS rules now prohibit referring to the protestors as "illegal". *(See Chapter 26)*

It creates an image in the minds of the public. Nobody wants to be called "illegal," so the IRS used the word to confuse the issues. Actually the tax is not illegal, nor is any protest of the tax. We have a right to protest anything and everything. But the IRS bureaucrats, like all others, are trying to make their jobs as easy as possible and non-conforming patriots do not help them.

If you want to be informed about rules and regulations that will affect you, your family, your bank account, your home, your car, your freedom to move about, your right to keep and bear arms, your freedom of speech, and all the other Rights most Americans say they value so highly, then you must read the words and understand the multiple meanings of each! You must listen carefully. You cannot accept things just because they sound nice or easy. You must "fact check" everything!

When you know that some official is going to make a speech, ask for a copy. Rarely do public officials speak off the cuff. Invariably they have a prepared text and they seldom deviate too far. It is the defense they have when someone tries to say "You lied to us," or "We were not warned." Whether you get the text in advance, or after the speech, skim it for buzz words. Check any statement that seems to be "qualified." If a Congress-man refers to a "speech I made on the House floor" – take it as a grain of salt. Ninety-nine times out of 100 they made no such speech. They just submitted the speech to the chair-person and asked that it be made a permanent part of the *Congressional Record*. But it is there in the official record, despite the fact they stated an opposite position while out on the stump gathering votes. Most self-serving politicians and bureaucrats are worried about being caught with their pants down so they keep themselves covered with an abundance of press releases, but you might have to read five different news clips to get the entire story.

In early 1968 I was in Washington, D.C., trying to hire an editor. The woman I was hoping to retain had a White House Press Pass and had to interrupt our inter-view to attend a press conference President Lyndon Johnson had called. After dropping her off, I took a copy of the prepared text and reviewed it at a nearby coffee shop while waiting for her. Then, listening to the end of the speech on the car radio as I drove to pick her up at the White House, I heard President Johnson announce that he would not run for a second full term. That infor-mation had not been in the prepared text of his speech.

Just a few minutes later, when I reached the front gate of the White House, demonstrators seemed to appear from out of nowhere carrying banners and signs. "Thank

God, The War Will Be Over" one hastily painted sign
shouted. The demonstrators and the press corps had
picked up on a statement in Johnson's speech in which
he stated that he had ordered "a halt to the bombing of
all non-strategic, non-military targets in North Vietnam," north of a certain parallel. To those who did not
study the text (that included the entire press corps and
members of Congress) it sounded like he said he had
stopped the bombing of North Vietnam.

The TV news media on all three national networks
(no cable at that time) reported it that way. The people
in the streets celebrated as if that is what he said. It was
10 days later when the Pentagon made an announce-
ment about current bombing missions in North Vietnam. The press was irate! The anti-war demonstrators
were angry! The President had "lied" to them! He was
still bombing targets in North Vietnam!

Of course, he was! He said he was "stopping the
bombing of non-strategic, non-military targets north of"
... a certain line (way north) in North Vietnam. I do not
know if he intended to mislead anyone with that statement, but I doubt it. The media did not listen. They did
not check the prepared text. It happens all the time. If
trained news people can get the story wrong when they
have the facts typed out in front of them, how easy must
it be for the average citizen to misunderstand. Since
then, there are now numerous cable-news networks and
the competition among journalists has resulted in better trained reporters and editors. However, other changes
in our media world have resulted in some serious checks
being placed on their reporting ability, like multiple
media owned by international conglomerates who can

set news reporting policy for the editors and reporters.

WATCH THOSE PERCENTAGE STATMENTS

Twisting words and percentages is a common game played by Tricky Dick lawyers, power hungry politicians, lobbyists, accountants, experts in every field, bureaucrat-controllers and unscrupulous media people who want to spin the truth without actually telling a lie.

Any percentage figure can and usually does mislead the intended audience. Treat all "percentages" as buzzwords to be scrutinized. For example: "Eighty percent of the majority considers the new law to be in keeping with the goals of freedom." Doesn't that sound like 80% of the people are in favor of the new law? But that is not what it says. The buzzword is "majority" and a majority is 51%. If 80% of the 51% favor the law, that is only 40% of the whole. Apparently 60% were either opposed to the new law or rendered no opinion. But that means the new law does not have the implied popular consent.

You should make your own list of "red light words" to catch your attention. Some key words you should have on your list include: rate of – reduced rate of growth – voluntary – compliance – net – increased average – gross – except for – adjusted for – despite the – notice of – cost-benefit ratio – mandatory - required – proposed - allowed – requirement that – permitted – lawful – unlawful – administrative – licensed.

Additional words that should cause you to read carefully especially when dealing with the private sector and investments: "plans," "seeks," "projects," "believes," "may," "anticipates," "estimates," "should," "intend," "best efforts" and similar expressions to identify forward-looking statements.

Anytime there is a descriptive adjective used in a speech, broadcast or press release, you should check it carefully. Everyone is inclined to embellish a speech or press release by using a choice word or phrase to exemplify their position more colorfully.

President Johnson's speech about halting the bombing of targets in North Vietnam should have been more carefully scrutinized by the national press corps. The people depend on this elite group of news reporters and columnists for information and truth. When the President qualified his statement with the term "non-strategic" the press should have noticed. When he gave it a further qualification of "non-military," our elected officials should have noticed. When he put in geographic qualifications, everyone should have noticed and there should have been absolutely no confusion about what he had ordered regarding the bombing of North Vietnam.

When George H.W. Bush was campaigning for the presidency in 1988, he repeatedly said, "Read my lips – No new taxes." Simple but effective – and misleading! His predecessor, Ronald Reagan increased the national debt by 250% by not raising taxes. George H.W. Bush raised that national debt by another 25% and added numerous government fees. Like Reagan, he just ordered more monetary credits to be issued by the FED. When the national debt is increased it causes inflation and is, in effect, a tax on every dollar already in circulation.

Half-Truths Are The Worst Of Lies!

Using the name of an innocent party in a story in conjunction with some known criminal is an easy ploy to sling mud. Try this half-truth for an example: You have just read most of an article about how one man was convicted of land fraud. He is, according to the story, one of the biggest land swindlers of the time. We will call him Johan Smith. The story continues:

"When Smith was checked into the state prison, he had accidentally brought a list of associates' addresses with him. It was confiscated and turned over to the prosecuting attorney as potential evidence in further investigations and prosecutions.

The media has learned from a reliable source that the list included the name and address of a prominent real estate developer, Bill Jonas. The prosecutor refused to comment when asked if Jonas was under suspicion of land fraud.

'He hasn't been indicted yet,' an assistant told the reporters."

This type of journalism is disgusting but it goes on every day. It is well-known by the media, police and politicians that the public is inclined to convict people by association. This tactic made Mr. Jonas suspect simply because of the way the story was presented. Someone in the media or the prosecutor's office obviously wanted to damage Mr. Jonas or the statement "He hasn't been indicted yet," would not have been made or printed.

Of course, you haven't been indicted either! The question should not arise. If you know someone who gets into trouble, you can easily be put into such a position and be considered tainted with "guilt by association."

Sometimes you will see the media used by publicity hungry detectives or politicians. Like us, they watch

TV shows such as the many cop shows or late night reruns. Some of our police officers are easily influenced by such shows. Some of them will occasionally go to great lengths just to get their name in the newspapers or their pictures on TV.

One sheriff, up for re-election, wanted to get some gangbuster publicity so he instructed under-cover police officers, borrowed from out of town, to take automatic weapons, cocaine and marijuana, along with thousands of dollars in stolen goods from the police property room and haul it all over to a building the under-cover cops had previously established to be a house of prostitution. To make sure the "pimps" (under-cover cops) would look really bad and arouse the dander of the community, the sheriff arranged for a juvenile prostitute to apply for a job and be in the house when uniformed deputies conducted a raid. With TV crews on hand they kicked in the doors and arrested the two men, three newly hired prostitutes and the juvenile hooker. They "found" a small arsenal of guns and automatic weapons, almost a half-million dollars worth of drugs and over $50,000 in stolen merchandise.

It was all true! The media ate it up and gave it top coverage. Child prostitution? Drug dealing? Automatic weapons? Stolen property? The public was aroused. They demanded the sheriff continue with his outstanding work. "Such people as these should not be allowed in our community!" was the cry of the media and the people. They might tolerate a few prostitutes and their pimps, but not child prostitution! Not an arsenal of automatic weapons! Not drugs or stolen goods! It was some time before the general public learned that the two "pimps" who had been arrested were really under-cover cops and the weapons, drugs and stolen property, displayed for the media, had actually been evidence in other cases and was placed in the house after being re-moved from the police property room.

Such activities as this are not always discredited. They are called "media events" and are very misleading. The biggest problem is that the public can never be sure if what they are reading, seeing or hearing is true or just a publicity seeking event. A spokesman for the sheriff's office never did say that the men were running a house of prostitution. He never said that they were selling drugs. He never said that the juvenile was working for the two men. He merely pointed to the goods and said "This is what was found in the house."

Eventually, the local media realized they had been suckered on more than one occasion and the reporters started asking the right questions.You, too, must ask the right questions! Read, listen and don't hesitate to pin someone down who appears to be skirting your di-rect question. If they can be devious, then you must be tenacious. Hang in there and you'll hang them!

Bureaucrat controllers and the courts can completely change the normal and generally accepted meaning of a word or phrase and you will wonder what hit you if you do not pay attention. My friend and his wife were taking an evening walk when they stopped to read an official notice posted at the corner. It said something about changing their quiet neighborhood street from a secondary collector to a "primary collector." Did that mean they would be getting more frequent trash collec-tions?

Being aware of government treachery, they called to find out what the term "primary collector" meant. After a brief, buck-passing, run-around, they learned that "collector" means "traffic street" in the bureaucratese language. What the local controllers and manipulators had hoped to pull off was to turn a quiet neighborhood street into a main thoroughfare with thousands of cars daily. When the people in the neighborhood learned about it (via interpretation from my friends) they all showed up at the next council meeting to stop the change. They, too, had not known what a collector was and the change would have been made if they had not protested. That couple did something just by asking a few questions and passing the information on to their neighbors.

When you question a bureaucrat, especially if your inquiry puts them against the wall at a public meeting, they will often resort to subtle attempts at putting you down. "I'm sorry you don't understand. If you would like to go over this is detail, I'll arrange some time for you. But now we must move ahead with new information," the bureaucrat says, patronizingly. Such a put down must never be accepted. This person, usually with some title or authority, has attempted to discredit your mental prowess because he (or she) is hiding something.

Do not start a war, but do not accept this tactic. Insist the speaker explain it to everyone, NOW! "I'm very adept at understanding. You obviously did not make yourself clear and I'm sure there are other people here who would like you to make yourself clear by answering this question, now," is a good stock comeback for you to remember and use if this happens to you. You not only upset the attempt at questioning your mental ability, you can garner some support from others who would be too intimidated to ask questions similar to yours. They do not want that person up at the podium to make them appear ignorant. You must insist that he has not made himself clear, otherwise the audience will be hesitant to support your search for the truth. When you start asking questions or making statements contrary to the official line, you are considered a trouble-maker.

***

CAREFUL WHAT YOU SUGGEST!

When I first heard about a Flood Control plan for a desert community where I edited a local, weekly newspaper, I felt as most people did — the streets would be flooded when it rained and the Army Corps of Engineers were experts about such matters. As I listened to a Colonel with the Corps explain to the city council about their planned project, I noticed he skirted some direct questions from a councilman.

Curious, I started looking into the project. Eventually I discovered that the plan would not prevent the type of flooding to which the community was exposed. It called for a multi-million dollar bond issue to be approved by the voters with several times that amount to be paid by the Federal government (also taxpayer's money). The voters turned the project down by voting against the bond issue.

At a meeting several months later, a General with the Army Corps of Engineers tried to explain their newly revised project to a group of interested citizens. When I asked how many times the people would have to say "no" before they stopped pushing this project, the General asked one of his Colonels to take me aside and explain the project to me (he did not want me to interrupt his meeting). The Colonel attempted to answer some of my objections to the project and when I pointed out the huge amount of money involved, he said the law requires them to show a 2 for 1 cost-benefit ratio on all projects.

That sounded reasonable, so I asked, does that include factors for inflation. "Oh, yes," he replied.

"Over what period of time?"

He mumbled an unintelligible answer and I repeated my question. "Over what period of time is the cost-benefit ratio figured?"

The Colonel mumbled again, but this time I could hear him say, "A hundred years."

"One hundred years?" I asked in disbelief.

Very few projects are good for 100 years. Usually they are outdated and a nuisance at the end of 30 or 50 years. If you don't think so, take a look around. The developers and planners are tearing out numerous projects that are less than 30 years old. With that bit of information made public, the next bond issue was also defeated.

When the Army Corps of Engineers came back a third time with still another project revision, they pointed out that the proposed bond issue would only add 5-cents per $100 of assessed valuation to the property owner's tax bill. Since the flooding was only a problem for certain neighborhoods, I asked why everyone had to pay since it was designed to protect homes that had been built in flood prone areas. The financial aspects were the only legitimate concern since there was no record of anyone drowning or being physically injured as a result of the city floods. Usually the water only rose a foot or so and ruined carpet and drywall.

Without a satisfactory answer, I pointed out that if they would pass a law that required everyone to pay me 5-cents per $100 of assessed valuation, I would gladly form an insurance company and provide total coverage for all financial losses from the flooding. The personnel on the stage just looked at each other. That was in 1966.

In 1968 the Federal government made National Flood Insurance available to property owners and in many cases it is now required that you have it if you want household insurance or a mortgage.

This is just one reason very good not to be a smartass and make a flip suggestion to a bureaucrat – they might act on it!

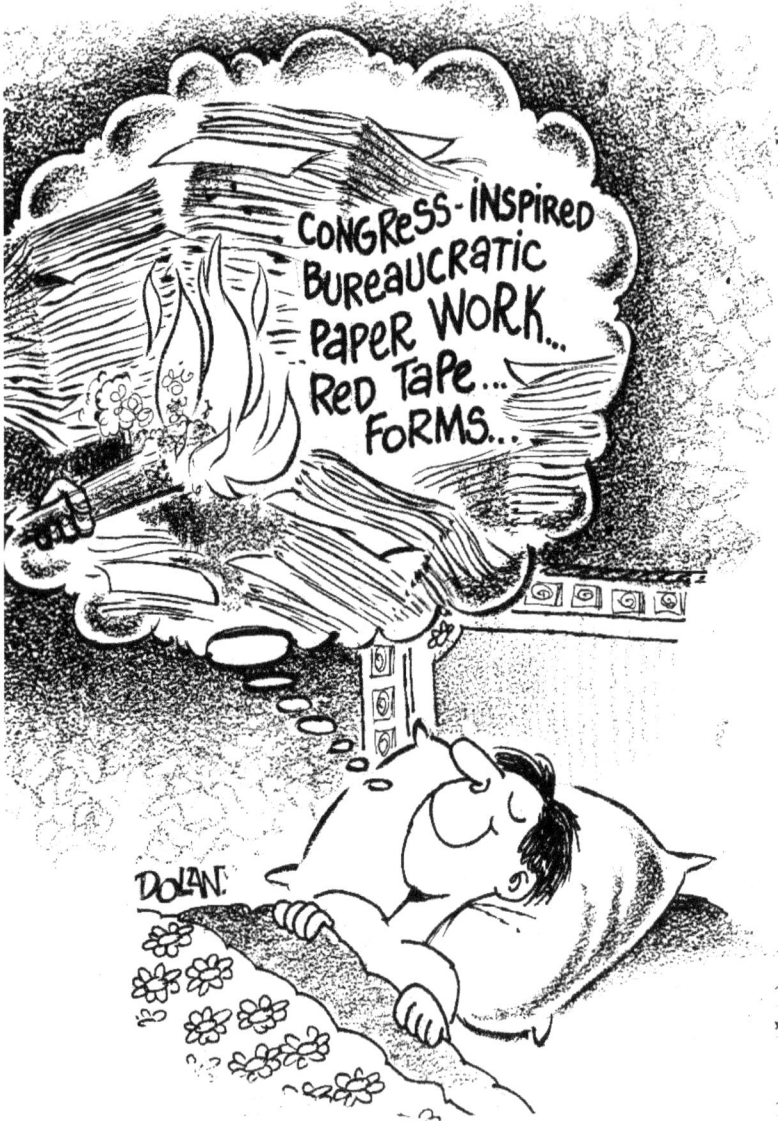

CHAPTER 9

MOTIVATION
Civil Servants May Be Your Tools!

A bureaucrat is an individual, elected, appointed or hired, who is often committed to doing the job for which they were hired or appointed. Most individuals who work for the government do not consider themselves to be bureaucrats. At the same time they no longer consider themselves to be public servants. They are, like most of us, interested in doing their job the easiest way possible, collect the paycheck, pay the bills, feed the kids and hopefully have some money left over for a vacation, college for the kids and a peaceful retirement.

The civil service employees, as public servants, are interested in doing what they must to keep their jobs and if there is a possibility their positions will be classified as non-essential, they will organize and fight for bigger budgets. They will say almost anything to convince the taxpaying public and the legislators that children will die and nations will fall if their agency is phased out or funding is reduced. Terrorists will take over if their budget is not increased. Organized crime will take control of everything if more police officers are not hired. All useful services such as trash collection and schools will cease to exist if there is a tax cut. Sound familiar?

You can make your own list, but before you criticize these people, keep in mind that they are not much different than you and your family - in fact some of them are your neighbors and relatives. What would you do if there was a chance your job would be phased out and you could do something to save it? It really does not make a bit of difference who signs the payroll checks. They put in the hours, do what they are told and get a check. The color of the currency is the same for government employees, politicians, bureaucrats and the private sector.

But there are government employees who will actually come to your aid covertly when they are aware of problems the conflicting or unfair regulations are causing you. That is, they can put the problem causing file at the bottom of the stack, save it in the wrong place in the computer or accidentally see that you get some information that can assist you in your efforts. You'll never know they did it, but it does happen. They are fighting back without jeopardizing their position.

The real problem bureaucrats are those ambitious individuals who go to work for the government and are anxious to climb the stairway to power and stature. They intend to advance and improve their position, even if the nation suffers as a result – they are bureaucratic controllers. They do not give too much consideration to such vague things as liberty, our national heritage, adhering to the Constitution or paying the nation's bills - unless professing such beliefs will help them get elected or advance their bureaucratic control and position of power.

When you hear government employees complaining

about being overworked, don't laugh. It is often very true. They are over-worked trying to comply with all of the nonsensical, multi-faceted, bureaucratic requirements of their jobs. Congress knows how foolishly government can spend money (they spend more than anyone) and they create buffer bureaus to write rules the government employees must follow, so they do not waste money.

Did you ever wonder why the Pentagon gets a bill for $865 for a simple ball-peen hammer that could be purchased at any hardware store for less than $15? It is the system that Congress has imposed on such purchasing to make sure the taxpayers don't pay too much! The regulation writers received their authority from your Congressman and in the case of the $15 hammer that costs $865, it is the rules that drive the price up.

When the General says he wants a hammer so the mechanic can fix the jeep — someone better find that hammer. There are about 20 pages of typed information that outlines the standards such a hammer must meet. A clerk must now take about 3 hours to find the correct info and type up the notice for bids, make several copies of bid sheets and publish the information.

Supply contractors' employees must now read all this information to decide if they have hammers that qualify. Since they will miss out on more bids than they will win, they have to add all the time they spend making bids and reading bid sheets, and then amortize their time to recoup the costs on the bids they do win. Cost of $50 per hour for the agent to read, times 15 bidder-agents equals $750. Cost of the hammer is $12, plus the $750 administrative costs, plus a 10% mark-up (cost plus 10%

contractor). The bill to Pentagon: $825 plus freight. Since the General was in a hurry it had to be shipped and handled separately - add another $40 or so and you have an $865 ball-peen hammer!

What happens when you complain to your Congressman about these ridiculous rules? He says there is nothing he can do about it. Bull! He and his colleagues wrote the laws that created the rule-writing bureaucracy. Congress approved the regulations and they can change them. Of course, Congressmen will have to fight with the bureaucrats for the changes. Civil clerks who push such legislation seldom leave Washington when a Congressman retires or loses the election. They merely get themselves assigned to another legislator and continue to slant things the way their friends in the bureaucracy would prefer – the revolving door of bureaucracy! And if you did find a truly concerned legislator, do you really think they would be willing to give-up control or influence over the multi-billions of dollars they each have as part of our so-called national budget?

When dealing with permanent bureaucrats in Washington, DC, keep in mind that they can play the waiting game: They wait for you to become discouraged and leave town.

Most lawmakers and rule writers are of the opinion that in order to do their jobs effectively, and provide service to the public, "the people must surrender certain of their rights" (at least a little bit of surrender). What they are actually saying is that they are not competent to do the job they are being paid to do.

Government's purpose for existence is to provide those services and protection to the people that they could not reasonably be expected to provide individually (streets, courts, police, prisons, etc.). When government controllers say we must give up our rights in order to have the service, then they are incompetent or are building a power base. Either way they should be removed from their posts immediately. They, like the politicians and judges, have taken an oath and swore to "uphold, protect and defend the Constitution." If they attempt to circumvent it, then they are in violation of that oath and should be treated accordingly.

What many government people seem to forget is that history is filled with stories about governments that have run amuck and attempted to take advantage of the very people they were designated to protect and serve. Even today there are activist organizations preparing for the downfall of the American bureaucracy. They are making lists of civil servants, officials, judges and politicians who have run roughshod over the rights of the people. Eventually, those on the lists will follow in the course of history and be hunted down, hung from the lamp posts or strung up from the nearest tree.

To better understand the extremes some government employees will go to in order to make their jobs easier, take a look at our prison and parole system. Did you ever wonder why so many people who are released from prison are back in jail within just months? The answer can often be found in the reports made by prison guards and corrections officers – all bureaucrats!

Parole Boards, in most states, consist of citizens appointed by the governor. They visit the prisons and have regularly scheduled meetings to consider the early parole release of those prisoners who have displayed an ability to "get along" in society. To make this determination these men and women interview the prisoners at parole board hearings after reading their individual files and records.

The records include reports filed by the prison guards, warden, various prison officials and employees. When the prison has to put up with a real trouble-maker, a guard's job is made tougher. He would like to have everyone behave themselves so he can get his paycheck and go home without a lot of headaches. The guards are going to keep reasonable peace, but they are not going to do anything to make their jobs tougher. Some of those prisoners are borderline psychotics who would just as soon stick a knife in someone's ribs as to cut into a T-Bone steak.

As a result, some "bad ass" prisoners are given plenty of room by most prison officials. If they want to shake-down the other prisoners or push dope, the guards will look the other way as long as it does not get totally out of hand and someone is killed. When it comes time to make out reports for the parole board, the guards are not going to give the trouble-maker con a negative write-up. That would keep him behind bars and a problem for the guard. It is to the prison guard's advantage to give bad marks to the easy going prisoners who should be released — they are easy to keep in line and the job is easier. Give good marks to the trouble maker and get them an early release — out of the guard's hair and back on the streets to harass society!

Enter the profit-makers! Some influential business types and politicians considered the question: "Why not open private prisons and take some of the burden away from the people and their governments?" Then they did just that - privatize the prisons!

While this industry grows and grows, it is not too difficult to find out who is behind the movement. Former U.S. Senators, bankers, state governors and even lawyers for foreign drug cartels are pushing for more and more private prisons. For most private prison boosters it is all about profit, but the drug cartels can use their influence (money) to make some of the prisons into a "perk" for their upper echelon pushers in the event they are convicted of illegal drug dealing.

The Case AGAINST Private Prisons!

There are many arguments against establishing "private" prisons in any state. But most of the questions are never raised. The way it is supposed to work is that private prisons can be constructed and operated at less cost to the taxpayers. Bunk!

1 - A private prison corporation must buy the land on which it intends to build the facility. The state already owns many thousands of acres and could build a prison without the expense of buying land. Construction costs are (or should be) the same.

2 - When a private prison is constructed and operated, it is done with the intent of "making a financial profit." The state does not have to make a "financial profit".

3 - When a private prison is built, the state has to guarantee keeping the beds (cells) occupied or pay the private prison for the empty beds. This puts the state at the disadvantage of truly representing the people since there would be a motivation to "lock 'em up" for non-violent criminals. And when the costs are calculated, it

leaves the state without the option to just shutdown part of a state operated facility if the courts and lawmakers decide to send fewer people to prison.

4 - Guards and security must be provided at any prison, public or privately owned. Do private prisons pay their guards less?

5 - Prisoners have to be fed in any prison, public or privately owned. Do private prisons feed the prisoners less?

6 - The total cost to the taxpayers in sending people to any prison, must include the residual expense of various forms of welfare being paid to the spouse and children of the incarcerated and the fact that the incarcerated individual would not be working and paying taxes. The courts no longer have those options with a private prison system and the committed expense of paying for the beds, causes the courts' hands to be somewhat tied! The taxpayers pay either way!

7 - To keep beds occupied in the private prisons, a state is often encouraged to bring in prisoners from other states. Private prisons are only allowed to house medium security prisoners. When California wanted to get rid of some of its violent "maximum security" prisoners, they merely changed the California method of prisoner classification, re-classified the Max prisoners as "medium" and then shipped them to a private prison being operated in another state.

8 - There are always some prisoners who give the guards and administration a hard time. In a private prison, they just ship the troublemaker back to the state as unsuitable. The state has to take the troublemakers into the public prison system, thereby boosting the costs

of maintaining a state owned prison. Now the private prison can validly argue that they can operate at less expense than a state owned prison!

9 - If our legislators decide to decriminalize some existing law, such as some form of marijuana, must they make a financial consideration that the private prisons would have empty beds - and that would mean the state has to pay for the beds anyway? Would the legislators be reflecting the desires of their constituents and what might be best for the state, or the desire of the private prison owners - profits?

10 - As a comparison, there are some people who believe that some doctors affiliated with certain hospitals will often recommend hospitalization of a patient when their hospital has too many empty beds. If the hospital is full, the doctor prescribes "go home, take two aspirin and come back in a month" - when there are empty hospital beds!

This is how the systems work. It is doubtful that you could find any prison guards in the entire United States who considers themselves to be a bureaucrat, but that is how they function. Until such a problem is recognized, solutions cannot be found.

Controllers want everything to be uniform. They must have four things to remain in power: (1) Information (2) Uniformity (3) Paper Work (4) Twistable Rules.

Deprive them of any of these necessities and you will win!

CHAPTER 10

WHAT COURT?

Threats & Intimidation You Can't Prove

Most government tricks and deception involve the use of certain words and phrases. Among these are the favorites, designed to get you to initiate action in court or to acknowledge the agency's authority, rules and regulations as actual law.

Almost every agency has some form of official sounding court or tribunal that terrifies the average person just as much as if they went in front of a real judge in a real court. You have the Zoning Board or the MVD Court and under the free trade agreements, there is a Free Trade Tribunal. The IRS has its so-called "U.S. Tax Court" which seems to have been the forerunner of similar kangaroo operations within other government departments. There are such things as "Administrative Law Courts" complete with "Administrative Law Judges and Clerks," — just like the real judicial courts. Even the U.S. Supreme Court has referred to the IRS's U.S. Tax Court as a "so-called court".

When the tax man wants you to volunteer for his rules, he tells you that you can either pay the amount the IRS claims you owe, or you can appeal to the U.S. Tax Court, or you can pay the money and then file a lawsuit in Federal Court to try and get it back.

Similar options are given by most agencies. You can do what the agency says, or you can appeal to some Zoning Board of Appeals or other formidable sounding body, or you can file a lawsuit in a court of law. Most of us are inclined to take the line of least formality. We usually take the position that our government would not intentionally do us wrong and, whatever the problem, it is just a mistake or the fault of some yo-yo who should not be working for our government. We opt for the Tax Court or the Zoning Court or the Appeals Division of the MVD, or whatever. When we do, we volunteer to abide by their rules and procedures. We enter into a contractual agreement with the government agency defining the terms. Then, if we fail to abide by the decision of that tribunal, the agency can legally take us into a Real Court of Law and have that real court uphold the administrative tribunal's findings. If we did not volunteer, the agency in question would use all manner of threats and intimidation (T&I) to try and force "voluntary compliance" with their rules.

The "court" you think you are in, may not be a court of competent jurisdiction! Over 27 states have amended their court procedures and levels to allow the establishment of "County Superior Courts" that do not have the authority of a "State Superior Court". A county court only has jurisdiction within the county and cannot issue writs, warrants or other orders. The "judges" can merely issue "minute entries" of their findings and then submit them for the imprimatur stamp of the State Superior Court. It is another Nazi-like system to confound the citizens and expedite the desires of the bureaucracy.

Don't be cutesy and think you can easily beat these

experts at their own game. They are masters of word usage and abuse and the courts try to back them up. You will have to listen and read very carefully. Next to the IRS, the Department of Housing and Urban Development (HUD) is probably one of the biggest abusers of implied volunteerism. Their rules (CFR, 24) state that if you open negotiations with them regarding the sale price of the property, "you have agreed to sell." The only question is the amount to be paid. If you say "Everything is for sale. I'll take a million bucks for my house," you have opened negotiations.

There is an old story about a man asking a woman if she would have sex with him for $1 Million. She thought a moment and said, "If I am to be totally honest, I guess I would have to admit that I would have sex with you for a million dollars." The man then asked her if she would have sex with him for $20. She asked pointedly, "What do you think I am — a prostitute?"

He smiled and replied, "We have already established that. Now the only question remaining is the negotiated price you will accept."

If you feel you must talk to a bureaucrat, keep a small pocket recorder handy or find out what app you must select on your phone to record a conversation. The few dollars invested will be well worth it to you somewhere down the line. Some states prohibit secret recordings of conversations and some will not allow the information to be used, even for reference purposes, if all the parties were not aware of the recording device.

Stick the recorder out front and advise the bureaucrat that this conversation is being recorded. You will be amazed at how much less T&I you have to put up with.

You will also be able to substantiate what was said, even if only for your own attorney. In the heat of what could be a hostile discussion with a government agent, we are often forgetful of embarrassing things we might have said and sometimes we tend to glamorize our position in retrospect. The same is true of government agents. The recording keeps everything candid.

If there is any question in your mind about the purpose of a meeting or proposal of government, then preface your questions and statements with "I'm curious. I do not intend that anything I say or my appearance here should be construed as voluntarily agreeing to your plan or proposal, but I would like some questions answered."

One way you might turn the tables on some of these tricksters is to make copies of the following Federal Law and hand it to them. Let them know you are aware that their program or methods are only regulations and rules, but these warnings involve real criminal laws that can land some trickster in jail.

There are numerous court precedents regarding both of these particular laws most of which agree that the statutes were, and are, intended to be used to protect ALL the rights of people and to punish anyone who conspires or violates those rights. The Courts have specifically pointed out that these LAWS uphold the Fourth and Fourteenth Amendment provisions of the Constitution and are not confined thereto. It is not meant to allow civil suits for such violations, although those may be brought under Federal, and some state, RICO (racketeering) laws.

READ THESE LAWS CAREFULLY! Keep a copy of these laws, preferably printed on business size cards,

and use them much like the police use the Miranda
Warnings. You can politely advise any government agent
or even corporate bureaucrats that they will be in violation of these actual Federal Laws if they attempt to enforce rules under color of law when you have not volunteered. Such WARNING CARDS are distributed at
cost by Survival Force of America.

Title 18 U.S. Criminal Code — Chapter 13

Section 241.

Conspiracy Against Rights Of Citizens

*If two or more persons conspire to injure, oppress, threaten
or intimidate any citizen in the free exercise or enjoyment of any
right or privilege secured to him by the Constitution or laws of
the United States, or because of his having exercised the same;
or*

*If two or more persons go in disguise on the highway, or on
the premises of another, with intent to prevent or hinder his free
exercise or enjoyment of any right or privilege so secured—*

*They shall be fined not more than $10,000 or imprisoned not
more than 10 years, or both; and if death results, they shall be
subject to imprisonment for any term of years or for life.*

Section 242.

Deprivation Of Rights Under Color Of Law

*Whoever, under color of any law, statute, ordinance,
regulation, or custom, willfully subjects any inhabitant of any
State, Territory, or District to the deprivation of any rights,
privileges, or immunities secured or protected by the Constitution
or laws of the United States, or to different punishments, pains,
or penalties, on account of such inhabitant being an alien, or by
reason of his color, or race, than are prescribed for the
punishment of citizens, shall be fined not more than $1,000 or
imprisoned not more than one year, or both; and if death results
shall be subject to imprisonment for any term of years or for
life.*

CHAPTER 11

FREE TRADE
Treaties Circumvent Your Rights!

The New World Order ballyhooed by President George H.W. Bush had at its core a new system of doing business internationally. He shepherded the U.S./Canada Free Trade Agreement (US-CFTA) while he was VP serving with President Ronald Reagan. That and all subsequent free trade agreements create courts that are beyond governmental or citizen control.

The US-CFTA was signed by President Reagan as one of his last acts upon leaving office in 1988. The House of Representatives passed a fast-track Implementation Act *(PL 100-449 - 1988)* to allow US-CFTA to become official. The Senate agreed! The agreement (a treaty) was off and running. A few years later NAFTA was created under Republican President George H.W. Bush and signed off by Democrat President Bill Clinton.

Those so-called free trade agreements are "treaties" and, according to the U.S. Constitution, become the law of the land. Those agreements create Free Trade Tribunals (courts) separate and above the authority of the courts of Canada, Mexico and the U.S. According to these trade agreements the rulings of the Free Trade tribunals cannot be over-ruled by any courts.

The rights of American citizens are negated by this

act. If a company, operating under the auspices of a free trade agreement, violates your individual Rights you can't even sue them. You have to get the federal government to do it for you – fat chance!

Jobs and entire industries have left the U.S. for foreign lands. And, almost as bad, the treaties allow for foreign companies to come into the U.S. and engage in activities that American firms and citizens are prohibited from doing. According to those "Free Trade" agreements, foreign firms can enter into individualized agreements with the U.S. government and its agencies and be allowed to do things like "mining" in a national park. Americans can't do that!

Disposing of toxic waste - foreign firms can do it, but Americans can't! Farming, food processing, mineral and oil production, banking, insurance, transportation - all are subjects of the "Free Trade" agreements and excuse foreign companies from meeting the same standards that U.S. based firms must meet. Even the due process provisions of the U.S. Constitution are ignored by free trade corporations. If someone is harmed by a FTA company, the injured citizen or state cannot sue them.

If an FTA company develops Genetically Modified crops and contaminates the non-GM crops in an Iowa farmer's fields, the farmer can only hope to negotiate with the FTA company. Under the free trade treaties, they don't even have to negotiate, but they will because it is good public relations – for now! It is interesting to note that the major promoter of GM crops is Monsanto Company (free trade) and they have thwarted any efforts to require them to label genetically modified foods so the public would know. Most companies brag about something they do that is "better" or newer, whiter or brighter - but not Monsanto.

California found out how expensive free trade agreements can be when they tried to ban MTBE, a gasoline additive that has been seeping into groundwater supplies and found to be carcinogenic. The product is sold by a Canadian firm that is protected by the US-Canada Free Trade Agreement. When California tried to pass a law prohibiting the addition of MTBE in gasoline they discovered that the Canadian company would be able to collect over $50 Billion in damages from the State of California. If the State wanted to go to court, they would have to do so in a NAFTA "court" and the decisions of that tribunal are not subject to review by any court - not even by the Supreme Court of the U.S..

One thing can be changed without negating existing business contracts! The President of The United States can alter any provisions relating to "Free Trade Courts" and thereby level the playing field for American businesses. The fast-track authority, given the Presidents by the enabling act, puts it all on the President.

The enabling acts passed by Congress that allow these free trade treaties to exist even include provisions for defining a "journalist" and such a person is not recognized by parties (countries) to the trade agreement unless they have been approved by their respective nation's Secretary of Education or Attorney General. That is tantamount to "licensing" of journalists and contrary to the First Amendment of the U.S. Constitution. But the media doesn't complain!

While many supporters of these free trade agreements boast of increased business for the U.S., the job markets do not support their positions.

The decisions of those free trade courts must be subject to review by U.S. and State courts of law. To prevent the loss of our Constitutional Rights in the future, we must adopt a Constitutional Amendment that protects the rights of the states and the people.

The seemingly harmless provision about authority to enter into "treaties" with foreign powers is being used to destroy America as we know it! Every so-called Free Trade Agreement (FTA) creates "courts" that cannot be over-ruled by any U.S. court. All foreign businesses involved in U.S. operations under a FTA (treaty) are virtually exempt from U.S. and State laws, rules, regulations, controls and taxes. Small businesses, farmers and property owners cannot compete when they have to obey the law and the FTA firms are exempt.

This is the <u>Self-Destruct Provision</u> in Article VI of the U.S. Constitution:

"This Constitution, and the laws of the United States *which shall be made in pursuance thereof;* *and all treaties made, or which shall be made,* *under the authority of the United States,* *shall be the supreme law of the land;* *and the judges in every state shall be bound thereby,* *anything in the Constitution or laws of any State to the contrary notwithstanding."*

After reviewing numerous treaties entered into by our various Presidents since 1954, with the advice and consent of Congress, this writer now sees how the tricks have been played and what it will take to prevent our nation from self-destruction, along with our unalienable Rights. In each instance the "treaty" creates an environment in which the foundations of our Constitution are steadily cancelled. The proposed amendment to correct this problem is in Part Two of this book. This amendment will fix it! *(See page 222)*

You can be for or against the results of any treaties, but the fact remains that, regardless of your personal position, our individual liberty, due process of law, court system and our representative government is being eliminated by each treaty – step by step!

Those "treaties" include every "Free Trade Agreement" (FTA) since 1988! More treaties of this nature are being entered into every year. Other treaties are being created that allow the United Nations to control private property, natural resources, government-owned properties, parks, the seas and fishing. Treaties are also being considered to reduce population growth by deciding how many children people should have – and who can have them.

Whatever Rights you hold dear, they can be diminished or destroyed by a "treaty" in accordance with the U.S. Constitution as it exists today!

Back when the Constitution was considered, the Pennsylvania delegation raised the question as to why there would be a Treaty provision that could wipe out the Constitution – no answer appears in documentation. *(Personally, I think Treaties" were included to cover the backsides of the American Revolutionists – just in case they ever had to surrender to the British Crown.)*

This amendment will not prohibit the government from entering into treaties! It will prohibit any treaty from over-riding our reserved individual or State Constitutional Rights!

CHAPTER 12

INSURANCE & BANKS

The World's Oldest Organized Businesses

Insurance companies are great at playing the power game in the U.S. and around the world. They have convinced everyone to be insurance conscious and have caused numerous "regulations" to be passed which supposedly require us to carry certain types of insurance. Insurance coverage now dictates how, or if, some of our traditional events will be conducted. Even the age-old tradition of showering the bride and groom with rice has fallen victim to the demands and restrictions of the insurance company. Fireworks use and public displays, reunions in the public parks or even where and how you park your car are all subject to those controlling insurance guidelines.

The insurance firms, banks, financial institutions and government are virtual partners in their many dealings. Bank loan customers are often obligated to purchase insurance through the bank's facilities. Insurance firms have done such a job building power bases that they have convinced city governments to pay millions of dollars in premiums when the city could easily be self-insured. Sometimes the insurance carrier is smaller than the city government it insures, but it continues to collect excessive premiums.

When small harassment claims are made by attorneys,

instead of fighting them to set an example that unfounded claims will not be paid, the insurance companies settle it for a few thousand dollars claiming it is cheaper than fighting. This opens the door to more lawyers filing more nuisance claims for small amounts. The payoffs do not actually cost the insurance company since they use such settlements as ammunition to justify higher premiums to their paying customers.

Then, to top it all off, some of these insurance company CEOs take a big portion of the premiums collected and buy "reinsurance" from privately owned insurance companies located in tax havens such as the Cayman Islands, the Bahamas and other offshore nations around the world. Those offshore insurance firms are usually nothing more than a desk, phone and maybe a secretary. The identity of the owners and directors is confidential, so the CEO of a U.S. insurance firm can actually buy the reinsurance from his personally-owned offshore company. For the company books it is a justifiable cost of doing business and is then added to the premiums you pay for your car, house, life, health and all the other things you want to protect against financial loss. The hospitals, and even your doctor, must pass along higher premiums for malpractice insurance by increasing charges for office calls, service and operations plus the costs of ordering duplicate tests to avoid claims that would raise their malpractice insurance rates even higher. You can be certain the insurance carrier will "lay off" a big chunk of those excessive and abusive premiums (profits) with one of those off-shore reinsurance firms.

The off-shore re-insurance companies seldom pay a

claim. The base of the coverage they provide is so excessive as to be non-existent. If the real U.S. insurance company does have to fall back on the reinsurance firm for settlement of outstanding claims, the "offshore owners" merely bankrupt their off-shore firm and start a new one with the same desk, different phone number and name. Since they are not covered by the multitude of insurance regulations requiring reserves, they have all their assets hidden so a filing of bankruptcy can be accomplished quickly and with only a paper loss while they keep the profits.

Stockholders and policy holders in the U.S. insurance firms should be looking at the operations of the company and if the records indicate the purchase of "reinsurance", they should demand a full accounting. Odds are that they are being ripped-off!

Insurance companies have created one of the most powerful financial bases imaginable. Their legislative lobby has caused the creation of regulations and rules which supposedly require you to buy insurance; laws that limit the amount of damages they can be ordered to pay by a jury; a means of sending money out of the country (beyond the tax collector's reach) and then invest it or loan it back to select firms and financial organizations with the stipulation that they help to sell even more insurance.

While the Affordable Care Act (ACA), also known as Obamacare, taxes people who don't have health insurance there are many controls the insurance companies do not like. The ACA put a bit of a crimp in this reinsurance trick when it required health insurance companies to adjust their premiums so that they are required to pay 80% of the money back for actual insured benefits. That only leaves 20% to cover operating costs and nothing for so-called reinsurance. But nothing in the ACA specifically prohibits considering reinsurance (offshore) as a legitimate, deductible expense. But that is only another smoke and mirrors trick! In 1988 Congress passed an enabling act *(Public Law 100-449)* to implement the U.S.-Canada Free Trade Agreement, and subsequently NAFTA, clearly exempts insurance companies from *"(B) any State law regulating or taxing the business of insurance."* Similar provisions appear in all so-called free trade agreements (treaties).

Many people started to become aware of the banking shenanigans when the "too big to fail" banks were bailed out with public funding (TARP) in 2007. Much of what happens with banks is covered in numerous books about the Federal Reserve and the public has only limited means of influencing the outcome of FED activity except to be informed and put pressure on Congress.

But the public can do some more things to put this 100-year old banking system in check. Regardless of how the FED was originally set-up to operate, it now operates in a manner even our elected representatives in Congress cannot explain.

While the FED was supposed to be the government's bank and keep private banks in check regarding the printing and issuing of paper money, The *Depository Institutions Deregulation and Monetary Control Act of 1980 (Pub.L. 96–221)* opened the door to allow the FED to issue monetary credits (print money) by buying private corporate bonds (FED calls them assets) just as if they were buying U.S. Treasury Bills. That same act allowed banks to merge and literally make themselves "too big to fail." Several years later Congress approved another Act to allow the FED to create that thin-air money based on any collateral bonds presented to them by "any bank" that had an office in the United States.

Almost every bank in the world has an office in the U.S. and is thereby qualified to pawn their bonds with the Federal Reserve (FED). The Federal Reserve Board has been "issuing" monetary credits for the entire European Common Market countries for over a decade. They are permitted to do this due to the passage of a couple of Acts of Congress:

1 - The Depository Institutions Deregulation and Monetary Control Act (DIDMCA) of 1980, which allows the FED to issue monetary credits (money) by accepting private corporate bonds as collateral.

2 – Another act of Congress, passed in 2006, allows the FED to extend such monetary credits to ANY foreign bank with offices in the U.S.:

Those who want to know more about the FED and how it uses double-speak, smoke and mirrors accounting tricks, to help Congress drive up the national debt and lend our national credit to other nations and their shaky banks, can read *"The Creature From Jekyll Island."* It is a best-selling expose' of the Federal Reserve System written by G. Edward Griffin. In it he unveils the background of the FED and the people who profit from it by creating money from nothing.

A REAL UN-INSURANCE SCHEME

There is a provision in an International Treaty which is now the law of our land This limits the amount of liability that can be charged to the owners and operators of a "sea going vessel" in the event of an accident. Subsequent Federal law *(Title 46, Section 183 of the U.S. Code)* extends the term "sea going vessel" to include all boats, even on inland lakes. What it does is to limit the amount of liability damages payable to an amount equal to the value of the vessel. The exceptions would be for intentional damage or knowingly failing to provide assistance after a collision and thereby causing the death of someone.

Despite this specific limitation of liability, many boat owners run out and pay exorbitant annual insurance premiums for boat "liability" coverage which is supposed to insure them for millions of dollars. The insurance firms love to see boat owners coming in the door. They only make a few stipulations: Your boat must be surveyed (appraised by an expert to establish a value); you pay the premium with the policy stipulation that despite the face value amount of coverage, all such insurance will be subject to international agreements.

Simply stated, the policy says the Million Dollar coverage listed on the face is reduced to the value of your vessel. The value of your boat should have nothing to do with the premium you pay for liability insurance. But it does because of that treaty which, according to our own Constitution, becomes the law of the land.

Then, to make compound profits, the insurance firms start loaning out money to marina operators with the stipulation that they "require" everyone using the marina or renting a slip for their boat or canoe to carry a minimum $1 Million liability policy. Those premiums for virtually non-existent liability insurance really do add up to a profitable bundle for the insurance companies.

Be Informed!

For those who think they can get all the information they need from the newspaper, radio, TV or their favorite Internet blogger, remember this: Many reporters would rather be covering sports. Often they are sports washouts who are assigned to cover such incidental news as political campaigns, the Nation's Capital, city hall and tax bills.

What everyone should do is to spend at least a few hours a week scrutinizing some of the legislation that is being proposed locally and nationally, but that is virtually impossible for most of us. What you can do is to read everything that relates directly to you, your property, your taxes and your liberty. You cannot blindly accept someone's version or "that's the way it is" philosophy of the news and expect to come out a winner in the power struggle. You can fight city hall — you can beat city hall — you can become city hall! Or, you can acquiesce to all the rules and be a slave to the bureaucracy.

JUST A REMINDER!

The power of the bureaucrats is great and they aren't going to surrender it easily. They will always find a new way to try and trick you. Remember: If you think it is wrong, it probably is — and you have to find out how the trick is being played!

CHAPTER 13

MANDATORY INSURANCE
"MANDATORY" —IT IS NOT!

Is it really mandatory? Don't you believe it! There is nothing mandatory about the so-called mandatory insurance laws your state may have on its books. Nor is there a "mandatory" provision in the Affordable Care Act (ACA) despite SCOTUS' obfuscated ruling. It's more of the double-speak word games designed to trick people into surrendering their Rights. The words and meanings have been so twisted around in our laws and courts that you can't even be certain that a person whose record indicates they are a "sex offender" ever did anything you would consider wrong.

To require you to show financial responsibility "after" an accident is a perfectly valid law! You cannot do harm to others and not expect to have restrictions placed on your subsequent actions. If you have an accident, the court can order you to refrain from operating a motor vehicle until you have made satisfactory arrangements to correct the financial harm you have caused, or until a certain period of time has elapsed. The same is true for the so-called mandatory provision of the Affordable Care Act (ACA). If you don't file an income tax return that indicates that you paid for health insurance, you won't be "fined" - unless you show up at a hospital without money or insurance. The "tax" (penalty) SCOTUS ruled was valid for the ACA will only be collected after you "voluntarily" file an income tax return with information that you volunteered. *(See Chapter 26)*

But, to require you to have insurance before you have been declared financially irresponsible - before you can license your car (pay the taxes on it) - before you can operate your car - before you need some form of hospitalization or care - that is "prior restraint" and violates the Constitutional limits placed on government that require due process of law and mandates that everyone shall be considered innocent until proven guilty.

You may never be involved in an accident for which you would be liable for damages. To enforce such a rule violates the basic precept of the Constitution. California courts struck down such efforts as being "in conflict with the Constitution" almost as fast as law enforcement officers tried to demand that drivers show proof of insurance. But the finding was ruled as "unpublished" by the court - another trick the legal system is using to prevent others from using the same arguments.

Other states have the same implied mandatory law on their books, but are reluctant to try enforcing it except "after" an accident. They want to keep this intimidating rule and hope it forces people to buy insurance. They are passing a rule off as a law and by doing so, weakening all real laws, the Constitution and the foundations of the entire nation.

The word "Mandatory" in the title of a law does not mean a thing. Remember the old adage, "You can't judge

a book by its cover?" That is especially true of laws —
you cannot judge a legislative act's purpose or legality
by its title. This proposed bill was given a title the media could use to erroneously promulgate a myth of mandatory insurance. Then it was given a sub-title to further mislead the public. The sub-title usually reads "All
vehicles required to have liability insurance." Following the Title and sub-title comes the body copy of the
law. That is what really counts. Titles do not mean a
thing.

If you want to entitle a law "Anti-Child Abuse Law"
and then draft body copy to make it illegal to chew gum
on Sunday, the legislators can do it. If people do not
challenge the basic authority of such a law, they may
be cited or arrested and jailed for chewing gum on Sunday. The court can agree to fine them only $1 and sus-
pend sentence if they will plead guilty. The person who
accepts such an offer and pleads guilty could then have
a record of violating the child abuse law and might even
be required to register as a sex-offender..

If you think that is ridiculous you haven't been paying attention to some of the weird rules and harmful
regulations being foisted off on our unsuspecting legislators, the media and the ever harassed public. Some
states have included urinating in public as a "Sex Offense." If a man pulls his car to the side of a road and
relieves that extra cup of coffee or beer in the bushes,
in the dark of night, and is seen by a police officer, he
can be arrested. If he is intimidated enough to plead
guilty to such a charge he will have a police record as a
sex offender The police or court record will not elabo-
rate on or describe the actual offense. Try explaining

such a record to a police officer who wants to know why you are parked so close to the school or explain it to your boss when you are being checked out for a sensitive position within your firm.

Many states are pushing the so-called "Mandatory Insurance" rule in an effort to curtail the numerous uninsured motorists on the streets. There is nothing wrong with people wanting to be protected from financial loss if they are struck by some idiot driver, or even if they are the idiot driver themselves. But almost every State still has a "financial responsibility" law on the books. That is a valid law that states, in effect, if you have an accident, you are then, after the fact, required to meet the financial responsibility for damages you caused.

Any thinking person will acknowledge that there is an element of risk involved every time they get behind the wheel of a car and move it out onto the streets. The risk is clear and constant. Since we are obviously willing to take that risk, why shouldn't we buy insurance just to protect ourselves against financial loss and forget about trying to force everyone to buy a liability policy? If you want to protect yourself in amounts that you set, you pay the premium and let the rest of the world drive uninsured if that's what they want to do. A number of states do have a similar type of insurance law - No-Fault Insurance. Liability would only be considered when intentional damage is inflicted, similar to the Federal liability limitations on vessels and on industry via the Workman's Compensation Law.

The primary problem with no-fault is that people who are uninsured will often require medical treatment and if the accident involved a pedestrian or non-vehicular property, that could be costly. While Florida and other states do not require liability insurance, they do require a person to insure themselves for medical coverage in the event of an accident and injury.

The solution is to do an actuarial study of the medical costs and property damage claims (other than the damage to vehicles). Divide that figure by the number of gallons of gasoline and motor vehicle diesel fuel sold in the state, then add that cost (about 7 cents per gallon) to the price of the fuel at the pump. A couple of cents more would cover damages to residual properties such as a pedestrian, fence or house that was struck by the vehicle.

A person who drives a big car will do more damage if involved in an accident than a person driving a small car. At the same time the big car will need more fuel and therefore pay more for the basic insurance coverage via the pump price.

Someone who drives 25,000 miles a year will be buying more gas and be more "at risk" than the person who just drives to church on Sunday — and they pay for the no-fault insurance according to the amount of gasoline they use, when they buy it. A man who collects old cars will pay for insurance based on how much driving each car does (fuel used).

So the government does not get into the insurance business, the premiums paid at the pump could be divided up among the various insurance companies according to the percentage of vehicle comprehensive coverage they are selling to the public. They would pay claims to hospitals and damaged (non-vehicle) property owners accordingly.

Today, when a person has four cars, he has to buy liability coverage on all four vehicles, even though he can only drive one at a time. Some of his vehicles might only be driven once a month. With this "insurance at the pump" method, he can buy insurance to protect his own vehicles against a loss and insure himself with extended coverage for personal injury and medical costs if that is his/her personal desire. But the basic costs of accidental medical coverage and residual property damage would come from the money paid for gasoline — the pay at the pump insurance premium!

People would be free to travel without the bureaucrats and profiteering insurance companies trying to convince them that they cannot drive without insurance (prior restraint). They will no longer be gouged by insurance companies who charge for every vehicle. People who drive more would pay more. People who drive less would pay less.

Among the major opponents of such a plan are ambulance chasing lawyers who want the deep pocket insurance companies involved in every accident, and the insurance companies who, despite their protests that they only want to insure safe drivers, love to collect those excessive premiums.

SOME RULE MAKERS WILL
JUST CHANGE THE PROCEDURE

When anti-smoking crusaders in Congress wanted to pass rules that could not be challenged in court, first a rider was attached to an appropriations bill authorizing the Federal Aviation Administration (FAA) bureaucrats to adopt rules regarding smoking on flights within the U.S. The rider circumvented the requirement that public hearings be held regarding planned rule-making that would affect a large portion of the population.

The FAA rules were first adopted to "prohibit the pilot from turning off the No Smoking light" on flights of less than 2 hours and later changed to include all flights under 6 hours duration (that means all flights). Those who might be inclined to challenge such regulations would need time to prepare a case. By the time they could get the challenge to court the question would be moot since the original bill's rider and the appropriations bill ceased to exist after 2 years or less.

Congressional appropriations bills are dead after two years and any money not spent is returned to the treasury or the general fund.

If the rule doesn't work - change the procedure!

CHAPTER 14

LAW PROFESSION!
Almost As Old As Prostitution

Why doesn't your lawyer tell you all these things? You probably don't hire an attorney every time you get a traffic ticket. Many people wait until they are obviously in serious trouble before they are willing to lay out money for legal advice. But sometimes you can hire a lawyer and he still does not tell you — either because he is not aware of some of the tricks being played with the law or he just wants the fee and you are not a big enough fish to cause him to do a lot of research for your defense or to challenge the rules. Their stock in trade is in knowing where to look it up and how to follow the procedures (rules) of the courts. They cannot possibly know all the laws and regulations. If you really expect that of your attorney, you should go on-line or to your local law library and take a look at what lawyers must contend with everyday.

Even the judges don't always tell lawyers everything when they make a ruling or deny a petition. Attorneys have been preconditioned in law school and beyond to admit to the superior wisdom of the high court justices. Young lawyers are awestruck and will often try to defend an untenable position taken by a judge, simply because he does not know what else to do. The judges are also lawyers and recent law school graduates know that lawyers must stick together to maintain the mystique and dignity of their hard earned licenses to practice the law.

It would be nice if you could be handed an entire brief of case law to verify the information you are getting in this book, but that would make it too simple. There are a number of court rulings at various levels which will substantiate the differences between regulations and laws. You will find them on every topic if you read very carefully and go back to *Square One*, but the rulings are not always obvious – you have to search. If they were so obvious this book would not have been published.

If all the lawyers knew about all the differences, the government bureaucrats and power brokers would not be able to use regulations to circumvent constitutional restrictions or Unalienable Rights of the people. The Supreme Court of the United States is very adept at keeping the double-speak game going. If an appeal is taken to our highest court and the question is not phrased in a manner that would allow them to give a double-speak answer, the Court will refuse to hear the case and let the lower court's misleading decision stand. This is almost always interpreted by lawyers, the media and the public, to mean that the particular law or rule in question is constitutionally valid. All it really means is that the question was not phrased in such a manner as to pin-down the Supreme Court Justices.

The numerous laws and regulations, adopted and amended on national and state levels, have become so extensive that law school graduates have to decide in which area of law they want to practice – tax law, corporate law, criminal law, family law, admiralty law, copyright law, or any of the hundreds of areas where it is essential that they specialize. When we didn't know that much about the human body, medical doctors could just be a general practitioner, but as our information increased, doctors must now specialize – they can't know everything! With all the conflicted laws and regulations, the lawyers must now specialize – they can't know everything!

But some lawyers do know the difference between laws, regulations and policy. When a Fox News station in Tampa acquiesced to the dictates of Monsanto Company, the major producer of technology to create genetically modified organism (GMOs), Fox fired the two reporters who had created an expose' on Monsanto's chemical treatment of cows. The report revealed that the chemicals used were causing cancer in humans resulting from drinking the milk.

The reporters sued the Fox TV station, basing their case on Florida whistle-blower statutes that protect employees from retaliation for reporting to a government regulatory agency any "employer misconduct" that violates any law, rule or regulation. The jury awarded one reporter $425,000, agreeing that the reporter's dismissal was retaliation for her threat to tell the Federal Communications Commission (FCC) about the FOX station's plan to report false information on television.

But the lawyers for Fox knew the difference between laws, rules, regulations and an official "policy." Fox appealed and the case was overturned. It turns out that lying on TV is not against the law. The FCC's policy against news distortion is just a "policy," not a rule, law, or regulation, so the Florida's whistle-blower law did not apply.

Although most won't admit it, lawyers are constantly in a quandary trying to understand why a higher court refused to hear an appeal which they were certain was valid. The thousands of lawyers dropping out of the legal system each year is evidence that something is wrong. Young men and women do not usually spend years going to school to study such a profitable profession only to "drop out" just when they should be enjoying the rewards of study and hard work. They are dropping out because they feel the system sucks — and that is because they do not understand the differences between rules, regulations and laws.

The Supreme Court (SCOTUS) does not have to hear every case presented to it. There are a number of legal clerks working for the court and they make recommendations as to which cases the judges should consider. Because of this procedure, these clerks are in highly influential positions. If they see a case that should obviously warrant a ruling with which the Court's clerk does not agree because of some personal, moral or political quirk, then the clerk will try to dissuade the jurists from considering it. If a case is brought to the Supreme Court with the wrong question (one which would most likely result in a decision contrary to the intended control rules) the clerk might urge the Jurists to deny a review and thereby allow a lower court decision stand.

The most recent procedure is for the government to trick a person into filing an action when there is no real or immediate threat to their Rights. The government then takes the position that there is "compelling government interest" — the keywords that say the other party "volunteered" and since the petition is voluntary, the person cannot show that their Rights have been violated. Subsequently, when the question is tendered to the U.S. Supreme Court, the high court will refuse to hear the case. The unstated reason for allowing the lower court decision to stand is the legal maxim, "Volenti non fit injuria" - Volunteers can't claim injury! But the jurists don't tell that to anyone.

The late SCOTUS Chief Justice William Brennan had something to say about the quality of attorneys. While addressing the American Trial Lawyers Convention in New Orleans, Justice Brennan told the attorneys that "Half of you shouldn't even have gotten into law school, much less graduate and be practicing law." He was critiquing their ability to write and express themselves succinctly.

Lawyers hate to take advice and opinions from laymen (non-lawyers) but some of the best courtroom and appeals "wins" resulted from a lawyer actually listening to a client and acting on the information. It was an airline pilot who insisted he should be able to file bankruptcy on an IRS tax debt. His lawyer, Phoenix attorney Ian "Mac" MacPherson, went that route and was successful. As a result you can now name the Internal Revenue Service in a filing for bankruptcy.

When Mel Fisher, who discovered the multi-million dollar sunken Atocha treasure ship, was prohibited from bringing the treasure up because his recovery device disturbed the natural ocean floor, I had occasion to meet his manager's girlfriend. I pointed out that the government was applying a regulation and how Mel could still go after the treasure. To make a long story short, the manager checked with Fisher's lawyer and he agreed. They started bring up more treasure.

Some months later, while CBS was filming some of the treasure, the crew dumped $300,000 worth of recovered emeralds into my special lady's hand so we could take a picture (she didn't get to keep them). Later Fisher's attorney invited me to address a group of Florida lawyers, but while enroute, he cancelled. Seems he found out that I wasn't a lawyer.

Whenever someone hires a lawyer, they should know something about what motivates that attorney. Obviously, they like to win and they want to make money, but there are other factors to consider. Most attorneys dream of the day when they can take a case and argue before the Supreme Court - State or Federal! In private they refer to it as "Arguing before the supremes!" But, with this as a motivator, a lawyer might not be representing your best interest in litigation if he sees that you have the money for such a fight and rather than win in a lower court, the lawyer "throws the case" but instills enough grounds for a very good appeal. Motivation and ego are key elements in a lawyer's profile and should always be considered when hiring one.

Foreign Influence On Our Laws?

Attorneys and judges depend a lot on the printed words of laws, even if they look for them in computerized data systems. However, most of the printed and digitalized U.S. laws are now being printed and processed in India.

West Publishing, for years the nation's largest law book publishing house, located in St. Paul, MN, moved its operations to India. Outsourcing of jobs is a major complaint in many quarters, but more so is the fact that the intentional or accidentally misplaced punctuation mark can alter the perceived meaning of a law.

An example of distortions appears in the Arizona State Constitution as printed in law books: In Article 2 of the original Constitution it states a person has the right to represent himself and the right to legal counsel. But in the printed books a comma (,) has been added so it reads: the right to represent himself, and the right to legal counsel. This has allowed the courts to misconstrue the State Constitution to require a litigant to "choose" rather than exercise both rights – self-representation AND counsel.

If this can happen when the law books are printed in the U.S.A., imagine what may result from printing our laws in a foreign country!

All laws are Acts of Congress, but all Acts of Congress are not laws!

CHAPTER 15

THOSE LICENSES
Drivers - Pilots - Other Myths

Pushing aside all the double-speak in the bureaucrat's rule books, in search of the elusive truth, we become aware of many previously accepted ideas such as a person needing a driver's license before they can legally operate a car on the streets or highways. That, too, is a rule — not a law. We might even call it a myth. The same is true of the popular misconception that one must have a pilot's license before legally flying an airplane. Still another myth is the argument used to promote "mandatory seat belt use" in autos – those myth advocates often refer to aircraft passengers being "required by law to use seat belts."

The truth is that you do not have to have a pilot's license to fly an airplane except at certain major, designated and controlled airports, such as Los Angeles International, Chicago O'Hare, New York's Kennedy Airport and several others. To fly the plane you must know the rules and you have a responsibility to abide by them for the sake of public safety. Contrary to popular opinion, pilots do not need to be licensed by the government unless they are flying passengers for hire or flying in designated controlled air-space.

You do not have to have a driver's license to operate a motor vehicle. Does possession of a driver's license make a person a better driver? Does lack of a driver's license make one less qualified to drive?

There was a young woman in Minnesota who tried to learn how to drive when her husband went into the Navy at the start of World War II. She paid 25-cents and got a license (no testing back then). She did manage to get the car moving in a forward direction on occasion. She was intimidated by the family car and refused to get behind the wheel except in an emergency. She estimates she drove less than 100 miles before her husband returned home in 1945 and resumed all the driving chores. She never got behind the wheel of a car again.

Forty years later she still had in her possession, a valid Minnesota Driver's License. Since she never received a ticket for a traffic violation, the state automatically renewed her license just by having her mail in a few bucks every four years, and having her eyes checked to make sure she wasn't legally blind.

Another man refused to submit to any prior restraints by the government and, as a result he has been driving for over ten years without a driver's license. He estimates he puts on over 15,000 miles a year and has never been stopped or received a ticket during that time.

Which driver would you rather encounter on the streets? The lady who cannot drive but has a license — or the man who is a good driver but refuses to apply for a license?

When you apply for a driver's license you are agreeing, in advance, to comply with all the rules and regulations the legislature and the Motor Vehicle Department (MVD) may make regarding that license and your operation of a motor vehicle. You are not required to have a driver's license. You apply for it voluntarily — therefore your rights are not violated if the Motor Vehicle Department suspends your license for any non-discriminatory reason they choose. You agreed when you applied for the license.

Prior to 1954 some states didn't even issue driver's licenses and most did not recognize the licenses of other states. When a person was stopped for a traffic violation, if the officer did not know that they were local, he would arrest them and take them before a magistrate who set their bond or fined them on the spot. The acceptance of a driver's licenses issued by a State has made the license a virtual "get out of jail free" card. If you have one, the officer will let you sign the ticket. If you don't have one, he will arrest you for the violation and take you to the judge or jail.

The problem is that most law enforcement people and judges do not realize that you are not a criminal if you refuse to carry around that driver's license. The driver's license has become a virtual National Identity Card. Possession of the license usually tells the officer that your license and Right to drive has not been suspended or revoked by the courts and whether you are local and would appear in court if given a ticket..

If, via due process in a court of proper jurisdiction, you are found guilty of reckless or unsafe operation of a motor vehicle, the court can order you to stop driving for a period of time and further order that you will not drive until you have passed reasonable tests of your ability and competency (MVD driver's tests). If you drive contrary to such a valid court order, you can be jailed for contempt of court. While you are under the court's jurisdiction (probation is usually involved) the court usually orders you to refrain from driving without a valid, state issued driver's license in your physical possession.

Until there is an actual court order, the burden of proof is on the government. You do not have to prove in advance that you are a safe driver before you drive. The law has the burden of proof to show that your operation of a motor vehicle endangers the public safety. (Warning: Do not argue this issue with a police officer who has stopped you. Save the arguments for the judge and jury).

The lower courts are continuing the double-speak game and have most lawyers and the public convinced that "driving is a privilege" and not an inherent right. Privileges can be revoked. What the courts actually say is that your "Driver's License is a Privilege" that may be suspended or revoked. It is a privilege offered to you by your state government which permits you to volunteer to accept the burden of proof and let them test you in advance. What the State giveth the State may taketh away! You cannot be required (except by court order) to have a driver's license in order to exercise your freedom to travel about in this nation by the most popular means of transportation available to you (your car) free of unreasonable restraint or harassment by government agents.

If you have a driver's license, your rights cannot be violated if MVD suspends or revokes it (unless you can show actual discrimination). With or without a driver's license, you are required to abide by the traffic safety regulations. The state passes most of those regs to protect the public health and safety. It has that authority and can enforce reasonable traffic regulations under its police powers. The purpose of all traffic control regulations is "to expedite the safe and orderly flow of traffic" and such regs are reasonable.

In fact, all those traffic regulations (stop signs, speed limits, turns, etc.) are based on one principle law with variations adopted in every state: "No person shall operate a vehicle on the streets and highways without exercising due regard for the safety and occupancy of said streets and highways."

The violation of traffic regulations are considered prima-facia evidence that you are in violation of the under-lying, primary law. However these are rules! If you came to an intersection with a malfunctioning traffic control light and it was solid red (stop) for all directions, what would you do? Would you sit there and wait for a few hours until someone fixed it or would you exercise caution and proceed, in an orderly manner, through the intersection?

When the regulations based on laws no longer serve their intended purpose (to expedite the safe and orderly flow of traffic), they become rules and each of us must accept the responsibility to use prudence and selectively ignore the rules.

There are regulations involving speed, stop signs, signal lights, signs, intersecting vehicles and pedestrians, when the public safety comes into play. Again, prudence is the absolute rule. If you see a huge semi-trailer truck, out of control, barreling down behind you and you have to violate the speed limit to get out of its way, do you obey the speed limit (and get crushed) or justifiably exceed it? You violate that speed regulation, unless you want to find out what it is like to be crushed under the wheels of a large semi-trailer truck.

If you own an airplane and don't know how to fly it, you would be a dead fool if you were to get behind the controls and try to take off without instruction. Any unsafe action on your part can result in a criminal charge being made against you in a court of law and the court can convict you of endangering the public safety — if that is what you did. But if you do know how to fly an airplane and you know the rules and do not fly in a manner that endangers the public safety, you cannot be required to have a pilot's certificate. The burden of proof still remains on the government, as it should be.

MANDATORY SET BELT MYTH

The seat belt story is equally untrue. According to the Federal Aviation Regulations (FAR's):

No. 91.14 FASTENING OF SEAT BELTS

(a) Unless authorized by the Administrator—

(1) No pilot may take off or land a U.S. Registered civil aircraft (except free balloons that incorporate baskets or gondolas and airships) unless the pilot in command of that aircraft ensures that each person on board has been *notified* to fasten his safety belt.

PILOT or PILOT IN COMMAND

The term "pilot in command" is part of the double-talk the bureaucrats have developed to further their controls over the public. A "pilot" and a "pilot in command" is not the same thing. The pilot in command is one who is in charge of flying an aircraft with passengers, usually for hire, and to do that you are required to have a Commercial Pilot's Certificate, a Medical Certificate and certain aircraft ratings and experience. Even then, the FAA does not require the aircraft crew ensure that you buckle up, but the airline's insurance company requires that they do this. All the FAR's require is that you be "notified" to buckle up. Of course, your friendly airline insurance underwriter certainly has some policy provisions that limit their liability if the crew does not require you to fasten your seat belt.

Don't misunderstand! This is not to say that seat belts are not a great idea — especially in airplanes. It is unlikely that you could find a pilot anywhere, licensed or not, who does not understand the necessity of using seat belts in his aircraft. However, the public is being conned into believing that government can make seat belt use mandatory in autos when they cannot even make their use mandatory in aircraft (except for pilot and crew).

Again, recall that a regulation is not a law. There are no exceptions to a valid law. In the case of seat belt use there are numerous exceptions for taxi cabs, school buses, delivery trucks, public buses — the list goes on.

The late Lee Iacoca, a former CEO of Chrysler Motors and once considered a serious contender for the office of President of the U.S.A., advocated seat belt legislation that would require everyone to wear seat belts while in a passenger car — driver and passengers. Although it sounds like he was concerned about public safety, his primary motivation was "profits". In his autobiography, "*Iacoca*," he pointed out that his enthusiasm for seat belt legislation dated back to 1956. Much of his emphasis was placed on the lives he claimed would be saved when people are forced to wear seat belts. But a few pages later in his book he admits that "such legislation could save his company many millions of dollars in lawsuit judgments paid each year because of accidents and subsequent deaths due to defective equipment." But Iacoca opposed the Federal mandate ordering manufacturers to install automatic airbags in vehicles. He argued that a certain number are bound to fail and then the manufacturer would be sued. But seat belts are not likely to fail and if people are injured who are not wearing them, no matter how unsafe the vehicle might be, the unbuckled person will be considered to have contributed to their own injury by not using the safety belt. The auto makers' product liability would be substantially reduced. Many advocates of mandatory seat belt use are not just concerned with safety. They are willing to violate the rights of the people by "mandating" an action. The purpose is somewhat self-serving according to Iacoca's own admission. Insurance companies have found that passage of so-called "mandatory seat belt laws" allows them a defense of "contributory negligence" if someone is injured because they did not comply.

After many state legislatures passed laws supposedly requiring passengers to "buckle-up", the National Transportation Safety Board (NTSB) announced that "people riding in the back seat of a car might be safer if they did not wear a seat belt." The statistics showed that people wearing lap belts in the back seat (no shoulder harness) are often injured more seriously than the back seat passengers who are not buckled up. Who should they sue? The NTSB and others had previously insisted that all passengers would be safer if they wore a lap restraint. Eventually the federal government ordered auto manufacturers to install both lap and shoulder harnesses in the vehicles they built.

Laws (rules) have been passed in most states that supposedly require everyone to buckle up. But they have been wrong before! Could they also be wrong about the front seat passengers? Shoulder harnesses?

My own mother died when she was thrown from a vehicle in an accident and her head struck the curb. The investigating officer said she died because she wasn't wearing a seat belt. However, he also stated that the lady who was driving, and another passenger, would probably have been killed or seriously maimed if they had been buckled up.

A young girl who had the distinction of rolling-over two cars before she turned 18 (rotten driver) lived because was thrown clear of the car and would have been crushed if she had her seat belt on in one accident. But in the second roll-over she had her seat belt on and it did save her life. The decision to buckle-up really is a personal one.

When you see a sign that says "Buckle Up, Its Our Law" there is a good chance that there is a regulation that requires state employees to wear their seat belts. That's legal! To order a private citizen to buckle up is not a valid law! Remember, if there is an exception to the "law" it is a regulation, unless you volunteer. People in taxis, on buses, in motor-homes, driving delivery trucks and numerous others (including children on school buses) are seldom "required" to wear seat belts. But, such so-called laws are favorites for insurance companies who want to claim "contributory negligence" if someone is injured, They know that about half the people will not be buckled up!

If you think it is okay to leave things as they are regarding the application for licenses and permits, keep in mind that such programs will always be expanded. Some states have tied the driver's license privilege to payment of child support or graduation from high school. Bureaucrats are seldom content with just so much power. They usually want to control everything.

Among the areas you can expect to see more efforts at "licensing" will be small boat operators, journalists, preachers and the kid who cuts your lawn. Everything must be controlled according to bureaucratic procedure. The enabling act passed by Congress to enforce the U.S.-Canada Free Trade Agreement (and subsequently NAFTA), provides that certain professionals working in a foreign country must have authorization from their respective Attorneys General or Secretary of Labor. Doesn't that sound like the start of licensing of journalists?

It should only be a matter of time before insurance companies will refuse to write libel and slander insurance for the media unless they meet the approval of all the Free Trade Agreements (treaties). The government is prohibited from licensing journalist under the First Amendment, but those insurance firms can make any rule they want. Not too many CEOs of multi-million dollar TV, radio and news organizations will want to operate with un-insured journalists.

In the 1990's, after several terrorist threats to airlines, the U.S. Government required the airlines to demand that all passengers produce photo ID. Nobody complained during such a crisis, so in 1996, the airlines started applying the edict on their own, demanded government issued ID, and blamed the government. The airlines liked the idea of making sure that nobody would be able to transfer the return portion of their airline ticket to another person. Now you must conform to carrying government issued ID or you can't travel on airlines. And following 911, Homeland Security has expanded all such requirements and even puts people on a "no fly" list just because they have the same name as a suspected terrorist.

In fact, the day when you will have to have a National Identity Card (similar to a state issued driver's license or ID card) complete with your imbedded Social Security number, is being proposed to Congress at every session. Legislation to supposedly help Immigration and Customs Enforcement (ICE) control illegal aliens will subsequently necessitate each of us to have such a card or passport if we want to work, cash a check or prove identity for any purpose. You are already required to have proper ID to enter most federal buildings, and without a valid passport in your possession, you dare not drive to Canada or Mexico – you will have a hard time proving you can legally re-enter the U.S.

Nothing happens all of a sudden - it is a step by step process of control conditioning!

CHAPTER 16

YOUR IDENTITY
That Social Security Number

When the Social Security System was created back in the 1930's, people objected to being issued a government number. They did not want a system like the Communists in the Soviet Union or Nazis in Hitler's Germany. They objected and the government bureaucrats assured the public that the Social Security Number "would never be permitted to evolve into a national identity number." To prove it, they printed on the front of the original cards: "For Social Security Purposes - Not For Identification."

Today, you cannot open a savings or checking account, buy stocks or even check into a hospital without a demand that you provide the service provider with a SS number. Your mortgage company wants that number. It is your Military ID number and it appears on most licenses, or is coded. Most states double-talked the public into giving it to them so they could put it on the driver's license for the whole world to see. After the Internet, computers and identity theft became so prevalent, they just require that you provide the SS number and they link it to another number on the driver's license. Often you can give your SS number to a computer operator and they can bring up your entire personal data file faster than if you give them your name, address, date of birth, mother's maiden name and ten other methods of identification.

When Congress passed the Privacy Act in 1974, it did have some good provisions in it. One was a prohibition against any government agency, which was not already using the SS number, from requiring it in the future. States and counties were ordered to edit all old

---

THE NATIONAL ID CARD IS COMING!

Solutions are simple to many of the problems we face. Only the incompetent person will demand that the people surrender their rights to solve the problem. The Immigration Acts were examples of disregard for the future effects of such laws. Congress has made it a felony for any employer to knowingly hire an illegal alien. Employers are subject to arrest and civil sanctions (arbitrated fines) if they have not secured satisfactory identification from each of their employees.

The only satisfactory ID will eventually have to be some form of National Identity Card. In the communist and other totalitarian countries they call it a Worker's Permit Card. In Nazi Germany it was a National Identity Card. Bills are being introduced in every session of Congress to create just such a card that American citizens will be required to have on their person and present on request.

public record documents that had been filed to redact (block out) all social security numbers.

Only a few states were using the SS number on driver's licenses at the time, but that changed quickly. Nevada had passed a "must" law which clerks were told to show to any DL applicant who refused to let them know his/her Social Security number. To further intimidate the people the Driver's License office had a big sign that stated, "No license will be issued to anyone without a verifiable Social Security number." Eventually Nevada and numerous other states realized their error and they stopped demanding that the SS number appear on the driver's license. Now they give everyone the option — but they still put the SS number in their file and if you know the numeric code you can determine what the SS number is just by applying the code to the DL number.

Some states merely indicate a place for you to write in your SS number on the driver's license application. If you do not fill it in, a clerk will ask you for it. If you refuse, he or she will innocently tell you that "you have to provide it." You do not! But to avoid arguments with the clerk you will have to request that the department supervisor be called. If the supervisor insists that it is "mandatory," suggest they call their attorney and ask about the 1974 Privacy Act. Plan to spend the better part of a day to get the license without providing your Social Security Account number. But remember, the driver's license is a "privilege" - not a right. Driving is your right and the license is nothing more than a "Get Out Of Jail Free" card!

When you are stopped by a police officer and your

SS number does not appear on your license, the officer will often ask you for it. He usually has a special place on the ticket (even warning tickets) so he does not forget to ask for it and write it in. You do not have to give it to him. He may attempt to talk down to you in an intimidating manner like he's about to arrest you or something, but don't worry about it. It would be a violation of the 1974 Privacy Act for a government (police officer) to make your Social Security number public information for any purpose. A traffic ticket is a court record and available to the public.

Fighting this might be a losing battle, however. Since government agencies are supposedly not permitted to keep your number on file, private firms are doing it for them. That is legal! Again, the intent of a protective law, passed by our elected representatives, is being circumvented by bureaucrats who want to control the people. Known as the National Drivers License Clearing Center (NDLC) it has a direct line patched into its computers to and from every one of the 50 states and the District of Columbia and, in many jurisdictions, police officers have computers in their patrol cars and can patch into that information. Whenever a drivers license number is available along with a Social Security number, both are entered into the computer. As far as the computer is concerned, your DL number, Social Security number and name are virtually one and the same. Since the FAA can't legally require the use of the number, they have the doctors get if for them when they give pilots their bi-annual medical check-up, and most all medical data goes up on some internet site or "Cloud" for recovery by anyone of authority.

If you apply for a U.S. Passport, you'll find a place for your SS number and an ominous "warning" that the IRS wants you to provide that SS number and failure to do so "may" subject you to a fine of $500. The Passport office doesn't care if you use it or not, and it is unlikely that they would ever deny a passport to someone who refused to give out the Social Security number. You are always "subject to a fine" and if it was a valid requirement, they wouldn't use the word "may!" If you apply for a passport and you do not want to give your SSN, do not mark or write anything in that space. Anything not requested in that space will be considered a form of defacement and you will have the government lawyers on your back. When you apply for a passport you have to provide satisfactory identification – usually a driver's license – and that information is shared.

Years ago, when a banker wanted to write my SS number on the back of a check I was cashing, I objected. I did not want the party who had written the check to have my SS number. He said he had to write it on the check. The dispute resulted in my pulling out my Social Security card (old style) and pointing out the printed words on the card "Not For Identification." That always worked in the past, but apparently the controllers had been searching for a way around that argument.

The banker, with a condoning smile said, "That just means we can't accept your Social Security 'card' as identification."

When the question of Social Security numbers came before the U.S. Supreme Court, the jurists again played the word game. They ruled that people do not have to provide their Social Security number to anyone except the Social Security Administration and the Internal Revenue Service. SCOTUS continued with the ruling and said that nobody has to provide you with the services you want if you refuse to give them your Social Security Account number! Of course, they are correct. You are not required to have a bank account. You are not required to have a driver's license. You are not required to check into a hospital.

Big insurance companies have succeeded in pushing for Social Security numbers to be issued at birth. To help them, the IRS passed a regulation that if you want to claim someone as a "dependent/deduction" on your tax return, they must have a Social Security number. When you apply for health insurance for a newborn infant, some insurance firms will only issue the policy and coverage with the provision that you secure a Social Security number for the newborn child within 10 days of birth. Of course, you are not required to take any deductions for your child, so such a requirement does not violate your rights. The trick included getting one of the most effective charity agencies, the Salvation Army, to require that any needy child for which a "Christmas Angel" star was put on the trees in shopping malls, must have a Social Security number.

Actually, you are not required to have a Social Security number. Prior to 1955 there were numerous occupations that were not included in the SS program. Today, you might find it extremely difficult to function without that number. Tomorrow, your children will find it impossible. Thanks to Congress, the bureaucrats have given us each a number to replace our name. Next you will find it on the birth certificate: A girl, 327-54-9873 was born on 03-06-15 to the very proud parents, 278-32-6789 and 438-30-6544. Place of birth (Zip Code) 55823. Attendant doctor was 432-98-6754. That sure will make it easier for the controlling bureaucrats!

Some people are seriously suggesting that when the children are issued a Social Security number at birth they should have it tattooed on the bottoms of their feet or inside their lower lip. Just like Nazi Germany, only a little more discrete!

Those who argue in favor of such big brother tactics can be somewhat convincing. Nobody wants to have the babies mixed-up or stolen at the hospital. Tattoos immediately at birth would prevent that. When the kids go to school, they will have to remove their socks and show their SS number or pull their bottom lip down to reveal the number. Those familiar statements "Open Wide" and "Bend Over and Spread 'em" and "Turn your head and cough," will eventually include "Show your feet," or "Pull down your lower lip!"

Your Right to Privacy almost always exceeds the rights of anyone to have information about you.

CHAPTER 17

MILITARY DRAFT
Of Course You Can Register

Young men turning 18 face a rule with which women do not have to contend. The Military Selective Service Act, along with Selective Service Regulations and an official Presidential Proclamation, requires (requests) the young men provide information. The supposed purpose of the Selective Service Act and the subsequent misleading material designed to "compel voluntary compliance" is indicative of these Rules vs Laws controversies.

The Privacy Act Statement, required by law to be sent to anyone from whom a government agency is soliciting information, accompanies the notification sent to young men regarding registration for the draft. It originally stated that they "are required" to provide their Social Security Account Number, but now the words "(if you have one)" have been added. Since there is no law that requires anyone to register it is obviously another ruse created to cause the public to believe that the government has a right to the lives and services of young men, despite the Thirteenth Amendment prohibiting involuntary servitude — slavery.

Why would our government create this system if it is only a rule? So, it can "legally" draft "the volunteers" into the military if some politicians should decide to embroil the nation in a war or police action. Since draft registration is not really a law, the young men are tricked into "voluntarily registering," and since they have volunteered to register, they can be considered to have volunteered to be drafted when the government chooses.

If there is any doubt in your mind, and the Social Security Account Number "requirement" does not convince you that it is a rule and not a law, look at the other warnings on the Privacy Act Statement: The information can be used against you in a court of law for criminal prosecution — that would violate your Constitutionally enumerated safeguards, under the Fifth Amendment, against self-incrimination; You have No Right to Privacy, according to the warning, since the information can be made available to numerous government agencies. Then you are told that failure to provide requested information "may" violate the Military Selective Service Act and "may" result in imprisonment and/or a fine. If it were a valid law, the word "may" would not be used. Obviously there is some discrimination in the application of the Act, so it must be a rule — not a law! All laws are Acts of Congress, but all Acts of Congress are not laws!

There seems to be reluctance on the part of the bureaucracy to try enforcing this Act except to let the future cannon-fodder know that they will not be able to qualify for government loans, government jobs or contracts. Student loans and other perks will not be available for them if they do not "voluntarily" register before they are 26 years old.

The assistance of various states is also enlisted to trick the young men to "volunteer to volunteer". When applying for a driver's license, the application in several states includes a notice that by submitting the application "I consent to registration with the Selective Service System if I am required to register under federal law." The app further stipulates that if the person applying is under 16 they will be automatically registered for the draft.

The current reward procedure is the most acceptable one. The procedure should and could be applied to everyone, male and female. Since involuntary conscription (the draft) violates the Constitutional provisions against slavery, paying or rewarding the people to voluntarily register is an excellent and legal alternative that was suggested in *"Break the Rules and Win"*. Citizens do not have a right to have the government guarantee their loans so they can go to college. Citizens do not have a right to have the government guarantee their mortgages when they buy a house. Citizens do not have a right to a government job or contract. If they want these perks, then they should do something for them.

Even women could register for the draft as long as it was clear that a call-up could include other services than military. We might find that we could eliminate some full-time civil service and some contract jobs if we were able to draft volunteers for a limited time to do some of that work.

This is not intended to counsel young men to refuse to register for the draft since that could be considered unlawful. The intent of this chapter is to give our young men and their parents the opportunity to determine the difference between a valid law that does not violate the Constitution and a regulation or rule that can be applied as law if you volunteer for it.

Voluntary registration with the Selective Service Board includes your agreement to abide by all of their rules and regulations. It is the same as joining the Army. That Master Sergeant has absolutely no authority over you until you "join up." At that point you become the voluntary property of the U.S. military and many of your Unalienable Rights are temporarily set aside (you volunteered) in favor of the military justice and regulations. To be a legal contract, you only volunteer for a pre-determined period of time — the term of your enlistment. If it was "forever," your agreement to surrender your Rights would be null and void. Since your Rights are unalienable they cannot be surrendered or taken without end. You cannot sign contracts for such a vague period of time as "forever."

Anyone who wants to be patriotic and serve their country in the military is to be commended. But every young man is entitled to know that he is "volunteering" and has not been tricked into doing it!

A Voluntary Fingerprint Trick!

The tricks are many, but everyone can thwart the tricksters just by paying attention.

A good citizen and grandfather lived in a rather high priced desert community and his house faced on a side street, rather than the street on which it was numbered. A local ordinance required that motor homes be parked in back of the houses — not on the side. Legally, his motor home was parked in "back" of his house when he parked it on the side.

A property developer and some bureaucrats didn't

care. They wanted it moved. They filed a suit in a JP court against the man and his wife. The local constable served them with a copy of the lawsuit and "an order" from the Justice Court that they both appear at the sheriff's office for fingerprinting at least 24-hours before they appeared in court. The man was confused and his wife was visibly upset! How could they order him to be fingerprinted for a civil matter? He called me and told me what was happening.

I knew that such an order would violate all manner of Constitutional protection and I couldn't see that community making such a mistake. The answer was simple: A service of papers by the Constable DID NOT EXIST until the Constable returned to the court and signed a "certificate of service," under oath, stating he had served the correct persons in a lawful manner.

Until such a document was filed, the subpoenas and order to be fingerprinted did not officially exist. If the couple went to a judge to have the order quashed, it would be denied since no such order exists. If they complied and went to be fingerprinted before the certificate of service was filed, they would be considered to have done so voluntarily. That is why they were supposed to be fingerprinted at least 24-hours before appearing in front of the judge.

After explaining this to him, I suggested he go to the JP court clerk's office and see if a certificate of service had been filed. The clerk immediately said there was a mistake in the service and he could ignore it. He then passed out the WARNING CARDS mentioned earlier. Subsequently the magistrate and the clerks refused to have anything to do with such proceedings!

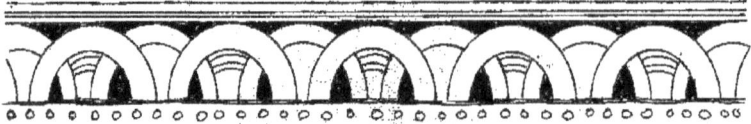

CHAPTER 18

FIREARMS
Back Door To Gun Control

Gun controls are being adopted at an ever increasing rate. The foothold was established using the popular back door approach mentioned earlier. Most firearms manufacturers do business with the government and sell arms and munitions across state lines and to foreign countries. Since the Constitution limits the government with the 2nd Amendment "...the right of the people to keep and bear arms shall not be infringed," the Bureau of Alcohol, Tobacco, Firearms and Explosives (ATF), formerly known as BATF, must control and regulate the firearms industry via intimidation and threats. Homeland Security insists on it and the original authority for most of those regulations comes from Section 414 of the Mutual Security Act of 1954 (and subsequent treaties) — the result of an Arms and Munitions Import and Export Limitation Agreement. It is a treaty entered into with other countries by the U.S. Government and ratified by the U.S. Senate.

According to the terms of the treaties, those who manufacture the weapons and sell overseas or to our own government, must agree to abide by the rules the ATF adopts to supposedly cause compliance with the treaty and any subsequent arms limitations agreements. The manufacturer agrees to refuse to sell weapons to anyone who does not have a Federal Firearms License (FFL). The Bureau of Alcohol, Tobacco, Firearms and Explosives (ATF), a division of the Treasury Department, will issue the firearms licenses to anyone who meets their criteria and voluntarily agrees to comply with the ATF Regulations. Either you will abide by ATF rules or the firearms manufacturers cannot legally sell you weapons. If you want to be in the gun business, you must voluntarily apply for and get the license and then abide by their restrictive regulations, designed to circumvent the limits of the U.S. Constitution.

You, as a private citizen, are not required to give any information to the gun dealer that would violate your right to keep and bear arms. But the gun store dealer has a FFL and has agreed to abide by the ATF rules and regulations. This back door approach to changing our system of law is actually causing our legal system to get bogged down. Little dictators want to force their particular likes and desires or standards on the entire population. The courts, sworn to uphold the Constitution, are permitting their authority to be diminished in the eyes of the people by permitting this back-door approach to circumventing the Constitutional limits.

If you want to sell your guns for a profit, you can do it. You do not need a license. Of course, ATF will try to convince you that you do. At a major west-coast gun show I noticed that a man had over 50 brand new handguns for sale and he was not taking down the names of the people who bought them. I asked how he could do this without violating the ATF regulations.

"I don't have an FFL (Federal Firearms License) so I don't have to follow their rules. I buy the guns from a person who has an FFL and I fill out a form for each one I buy. What I do with it after that is none of the government's business," he explained. The guns were all a part of his "private collection." He collected new, unfired, automatic pistols — no two were alike. When he decided to sell his collection at a profit, he didn't violate the rules. Free enterprise in action! However, don't count on it! Those who want to disarm America are actively looking for ways to require private citizens to run checks on buyers or be held financially responsible for anything the subsequent buyers do with the gun.

The Federal Firearms License Application *(CFR 55.45)* is submitted "under penalty of perjury and the penalties imposed by 18 USC 844(a)." Such a phrase and threat would not be necessary if it were really a valid requirement that dealers have a license. A valid law can speak for itself. Rules need a tangled web of deceit, red tape and back-up regulations to keep from falling apart under close scrutiny or challenge.

It is also interesting to note when reading the CFR manuals, that there is continued references to laws, treaties and other regulations. This is usually a successful method of discouraging the public and lawyers from searching too far. You can only crack so many books or review so much on the Internet in attempts to find the correct answer. Eventually the cross references can get one to the point where you forget the original question.

Many fascist controls are being put into place all the time. It is a violation of OSHA regulations for a licensed garage to do mechanical work on a car when the emissions equipment has been disconnected or removed. The

Feds coerced the states to pass such regulations or face the possibility of "losing highway funding." Successful application of such controls will eventually lead to more and more controls.

In a Supreme Court decision regarding search warrants for "closely regulated" businesses (firearms, liquor, etc.), the Court actually held that because the industry is so closely regulated and controlled, they have no right to expect any privacy and therefore search warrants are not required:

"...when an entrepreneur embarks upon such a business, he has voluntarily chosen to subject himself to a full arsenal of government regulation." *(Marshall v. Barlow's, Inc., supra, 98 Supreme Court at 1820-21).* Note the ruling used the word "voluntarily"!

How long will it be before the Supreme Court decides that since "We the people..." have been so closely regulated in the past, that we can no longer have an expectation of our Right to keep and bear arms or a Right to privacy?

Looking back on history, people are not enslaved until they have been disarmed. Taking weapons from the citizenry was the first act of Hitler's Nazis when they invaded any country. Attempts to disarm the American people are often thwarted but it is happening very gradually. Giving a rifle the description of being an "assault rifle" simply because that is the military term for a semi-automatic rifle, is one step to condition the public to ban them. Limiting the size of magazines or gun clips to 20 or 10 or 5 might sound reasonable to some of the population, but once the government's foot is in the door, it is only a matter of time before laws are adopted that say the weapon can only carry a single-shot. That wouldn't be a defense if 3 masked men invaded your house.

It was surprising that conservative President Ronald Reagan signed an Executive Order prohibiting citizens from carrying firearms in any National Park and it was liberal President Barack Obama who rescinded that EO and restored the right of citizens to carry firearms in the National Parks as a means of defending themselves from wild animals - but no hunting.

While the anti-gun advocates continue their crusade "to save lives" by ignoring the 2nd Amendment's limitation of "shall not be infringed", the nation will slowly be disarmed, controlled and then subject to the whims of whatever politicians take control of the government.

STOP PROFITS FROM ILLEGAL DRUGS

Solutions can also be found to curb illegal drug smuggling and abuse. The problem can be solved by legalizing and controlling the use of the drugs at affordable prices. When the huge profits are removed, few will be inclined to "push" the drugs to school kids. People who are addicted will not have to rob and steal to get their daily fix — they can work and buy their "fix" at the drug store or get their injections from a physician.

Firearms are used as a barter system to trade for "controlled substances" (drugs) and then those guns are used to facilitate more drug smuggling - because the drugs are illegal! The answer for some anti-gun activists is to ban the guns and keep the drugs illegal. Those dealers in illegal drugs are already breaking the law, what do they care if you make the guns illegal? They don't seem to have read their history about the days when we had prohibition of alcohol.

Another solution to preserve our rights by decriminalizing illegal drugs is to turn all the old military bases into paradise for addicts. Let them come on the base and have all the drugs they want with just a few stipulations: They make out their Last Will & Testament; they watch a short movie showing them what can happen if they get all the drugs they want; they acknowledge an alternative service that is offered to help them get clean; they acknowledge that they will have a smorgasbord of drugs and if they over-dose, there will be no care given — they will be allowed to die. The only way they leave is dead or take the cure and be clean!

The real solution is to take the profits out of drugs. Thousands of men and women have fought wars and died to preserve our Rights and liberty. Now we are expected to surrender those Rights because some pusher or lawyer or corrupt politician wants a profit and some jerk wants to take the drugs — let some drug addicts die to preserve our Rights!

With all the billions of dollars spent since 1954, when the Drug Enforcement Administration (DEA) was formed, and all the man-power wasted, the problem has not been solved. It is actually worse today. Big Brother controls on the legal monetary activity and the movements of citizens is not the answer. Not only has the drug problem grown, many of the Drug Enforcement Agents (working undercover) have helped it to grow and have reaped huge profits from it. You cannot have all that money floating around without corrupting the police, judges, politicians and the entire "justice" system.

At the time the DEA was formed in 1954 there were 25,000 known drug addicts in the U.S.. Most were musicians, former hospital patients and doctors.

Everyone is anxious to stop criminal activity, but when the illegal drug industry is responsible for more than 50% of all property crimes and murders, and over half of all convicts in our prisons it becomes obvious that we need a different approach...

...or continue to surrender our Rights!

THINK ABOUT IT!

A former DEA supervisor retired after 25 years and wrote a revealing book about his last under-cover operation. *"Deep Cover"* was written by Michael Levine and gives the inside story of the incompetence and subterfuge of our government to continue the war on drugs.

His conclusion is that we have no intention of winning that "war" - it is much too profitable for too many people!

Next time you see a news report of some crime being committed, ask this question: "Would that crime have taken place if drugs were legal?"

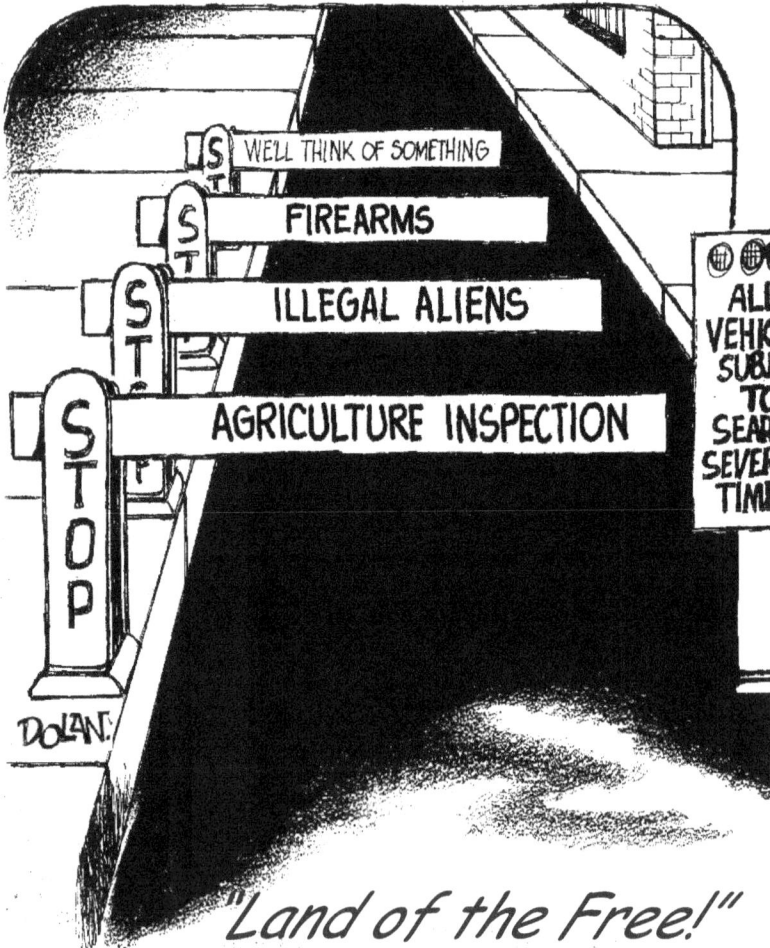

CHAPTER 19

CHECKPOINTS
Without A Search Warrant?

It sounds repetitious but it bears repeating: The Constitution limits the actions of Government. All authority and Rights not specifically granted to the Federal government belong to the people, or to the States to which the people have delegated limited authority. Those reserved Rights include being free from unreasonable search and seizure — to be secure in one's person and papers. This puts a limit on when and how the government can search us or our property. Search warrants are required in most instances and can only be issued by a magistrate (judge) of competent jurisdiction.

Search warrants must specify those things to be searched and the items expected to be found and seized during the search. Such warrants are only issued in criminal cases and someone, under penalty of perjury, must swear they have reasonable cause to believe that the incriminating items will be found at the location to be searched. Officers may also conduct reasonable searches of a person when making an arrest to ascertain the arrestee is not armed or carrying dangerous items or contraband.

If anyone tries to tell you that there is no guarantee of privacy in the Constitution, remind them of the Fourth

Amendment's provision of the "right to be secure in one's person and papers." You cannot be "secure" if you don't have a right to be private, secret or unexposed. Security of any type automatically means private!

With this in mind, one must ask how a state agricultural agent can get a "search warrant" to look for the gypsy moth in a car or camper traveling into California from Oregon? How can the Immigration and Customs (ICE) or Customs and Border Protection (CBP) get authority to stop you on an Interstate Highway, 40 miles from the U.S./Mexico border and look your car over to decide if you might be hauling illegal aliens? How can a game warden search your vehicle looking for too many fish or some animal a hunter has shot? Unless a State of Emergency is declared or they have probable cause — or you volunteer to be searched - they cannot! The key word, again, is VOLUNTEER!

You have a right to travel about freely in this country, from state to state, without harassment and interference by the government. Some bureaucrats do not care how many individual rights have to be twisted and circumvented to accomplish their tasks. For these purposes they have created, with consent of the U.S. Supreme Court, a thing called "Administrative Search Warrants". Like the Administrative Courts the bureaucrats established to assist in controlling and intimidating the public, the Administrative Search Warrants require your voluntary cooperation or they would be in violation of the Constitution. Again, the rule is that you have to appear to volunteer for any such searches.

Even your state fish and game department gets in on

the act. In the case of the game warden, when you purchased your hunting or fishing license you agreed to comply with the game warden's request to inspect your private property to make sure you are in compliance with the rules of the fish and game department.

To cause you to volunteer without actually violating the law the INS, ICE, CBP and the other regulators and law enforcement groups have feigned following SCOTUS guidelines and established some fixed checkpoints on state highways and the Interstate system. The Court ruled that the check points cannot be open all the time and there must be alternate routes for the public to take. In this way, the motoring public can be concluded to have "voluntarily driven the route where the checkpoint is established." Since you are there, you volunteered to let them "look you over." If the officers have any reasonable cause, they can ask you questions and check you out at a secondary inspection, just as if you had just crossed the border into the United States from a foreign country – Canada or Mexico.

They can legally tell you that they have a search warrant and suggest that it is better if you volunteer to open your trunk. What they do not say is that the search warrant is "Administrative" and it requires your voluntary cooperation to make it effective. Many of these so-called search warrants have printed on the cover "Compliance Is Required." Again, those words mean: "Voluntary Compliance is Requested."

Do not misunderstand — the immigration, customs and agriculture people have every right to inspect and search when someone is entering the United States from another country. It is only after one is here that there is limited authority which is being abused. All law enforcement and similar agencies must have "reasonable cause" to stop anyone driving down an Interstate freeway, even when they have not been out of the country — unless the subject volunteers.

Along the Mexican border the border patrol is putting on more and more manpower to supposedly try and stem the flood of illegal aliens entering the country to "take away our jobs." If anyone is really concerned that illegal aliens might be taking American jobs, take a close look at where your car was manufactured. Where did your shirt come from? Who made your watch? Your cell phone or iPad? Your TV set? Camera? We export far more jobs by buying foreign made products than those illegal aliens could ever take away.

To try and reduce the numbers who successfully make it up north where they can find work, ICE and Border Patrol has established several permanent check points along the U.S. Interstate freeways in states bordering Mexico. Thousands of U.S. citizens are subjected to warning signs, orange directional pylons and "STOP" signs at these locations, as they drive on the highways in their own country.

Those intimidating orange pylons are placed across the highway, but not by the State Highway Department or the police. The pylons are placed, like the signs, by ICE agents to direct traffic off the highway and into their inspection stations. In some instances, the motorist is only required to drive very slowly and is waved on before they even bring their vehicle to a complete stop. The agent merely looks at your face and is supposed to determine from this if you are an illegal alien or a "coyote" (alien smuggler). This process is supposed to assist ICE in apprehending illegal aliens and most Americans accept this restriction of their liberty as "a small violation" to suffer so the illegal alien problem can be resolved. More recently, the agents stop almost every vehicle and ask some question like, "Where are you going?" so they can determine if you have a foreign accent.

But the problem is not being resolved! People are merely being conditioned to accept more and more government controls over their lives. They are being programmed to accept more "small violations" of the Constitution and their Rights.

What is truly amazing is the way the U.S. Supreme Court ruled in "allowing" these road blocks. The Jurists acknowledged that the stops "do constitute seizure" according to the Fourth Amendment, but they would "allow" them with certain restrictions!

Allow? Who gave the Supreme Court authority to "allow" a violation of the Constitution? But, the High Court Justices seem to feel that the violations of citizen rights with checkpoints is a lesser evil than having Border Patrol officers stopping suspicious vehicles at random — which the Judges had previously declared illegal. To accomplish this end, SCOTUS said the roadblocks can be erected provided there is an alternate way to go around them and/or specific hours of operation.

The Governors of each state where these checkpoints are established could order them removed from the state controlled highways and rights of way. ICE is abusing the police powers of the states by putting up traffic pylons and STOP signs along the highways. State government is responsible for establishing traffic control on all of its roads and highways. The Federal government has no such authority. It can be a great power tool that state governments can use to whip the federal bureaucrats into submission. The federal bureaucrats will play their wily tricks on everyone, if they can. One person, city, county or state, out of sync with the Washington drum beat will cause the Feds to change their tempo. It never fails!

I decided to challenge the stop procedure at one check point on Interstate 10, about 40 miles from El Paso, TX, and the U.S.-Mexican border. The three INS officers I spoke with tried to justify such stops with double-talk figures of 100,000 illegal aliens, and then 30,000 illegal aliens being apprehended. Eventually, they admitted that their particular checkpoint only resulted in the arrests of 10 to 12 illegal aliens a week. It takes 20 full-time Border Patrol/ICE agents to man that station. The arrest rate of illegals at that Las Cruces, N.M., checkpoint amounted to less than one per agent per week. They could do better on horseback riding along the border instead of violating the rights of U.S. motorists as they drive down the freeways they paid for with gasoline taxes.

Then those officers acknowledged that some of the illegals were OTM's (Other Than Mexican) that ICE had detained at the checkpoint. Some of those 10 or 12 illegal aliens they captured each week were British, French, Italian, German, or some other visitors or students who had "overstayed their visas." The visiting privileges could have been renewed very easily if the visitors had noticed. Since the visas were not renewed, the government "caught some real illegal aliens" in their roadblock-checkpoint. One immigration agent displayed the typical bureaucrat attitude with the comment, "It may not be the original Bill of Rights, but what is anymore?"

When the Supreme Court ruled that the check points must not be operated continuously and there must be an alternate route to avoid the checkpoint, those Jurists rationalized that we could then be considered to have "voluntarily driven into these checkpoints" *(See Court Ruling U.S. v Martinez-Fuerte).*

I decided to try driving the alternate route around the busiest of these roadblocks on Interstate 5 between San Diego and Los Angeles. The alternate route took almost three extra hours driving over unimproved back roads. After about 15 miles of driving on winding dirt roads, I ended up on Interstate 15, just north of another checkpoint. True, I had managed to retain my right to travel without being harassed by government roadblocks, but I do not consider driving 3 hours and over 15 miles out of the way, and an extra 40 miles to get to my destination as a "reasonable" alternative to volunteering for the roadblocks.

In the arguments to substantiate the need for such road blocks as a "compelling government interest", the government said that if everyone had to drive slow, as they do on the back highways and roads, the officers could look the vehicles and occupants over without having to stop them. During the 15-mile jaunt on some very scenic, but rough, back roads, not one immigration patrol car was found. The big motor-home I was driving could have been loaded with illegal Mexican aliens or OTMs, and not one agent was to be found — except at the Checkpoints "voluntarily" entered by U.S. citizens and a few really un-informed aliens who do not know the back road is free of government agents.

It is doubtful that there is one Supreme Court jurist who can honestly say that such a circuitous route, more than 40 miles out of the way, does not violate the rights of the people to travel, free of government interference. Illegal aliens may be a serious problem, but the Big Brother checkpoints do not solve the problem. The numbers migrating into the U.S. have increased dramatically over the many years those control stations have been hassling American citizens.

Since that SCOTUS ruling, the checkpoints are no longer just "temporary" trailers – permanent structures have been built and I would challenge anyone to find a way around them or get a list of operating hours. I tried both methods several years after the SCOTUS ruling and found the alternate old roads were blocked or eliminated and when I requested hours of operation, I received no response.

Every ICE roadblock is violating the 14th Amendment as SCOTUS had stated and there are no alternate routes or published hours of operation. Those justices advised a system whereby the government could trick the public into "volunteering" to avoid violation of the 14th Amendment. Then, with everyone convinced that Starre Decisis would prevail, the alternate routes and times of operation suggested by SCOTUS were totally ignored. But nobody wants to raise the question again!

But the procedure doesn't stop with ICE and other federal agents. City police, County Sheriffs and Highway Patrol are taking the cue and setting up unannounced roadblocks to apprehend drivers who have been drinking alcoholic beverages.

Nobody wants drunk drivers on the road! But, unless there is advanced notice of a roadblock (which most drunks wouldn't notice) and an alternate route, such stops are violating the Rights of the sober motoring public and in direct violation of the SCOTUS procedure ruling.

In order to be "driving under the influence" (DUI), it is only necessary to admit you have had one beer - you are under the influence! There is also a question of whether these stops are to protect public health and safety or are they an excuse for revenue enhancement?

When MADD (Mothers Against Drunk Driving) lawyers lobby the legislators to continually reduce the blood alcohol level and get it down to .08 it is easy to say the driver is Driving While Intoxicated (DWI) and it appears to be more for revenue enhancement purposes than for public safety. Just one drink means you are operating "under the influence"! A healthy woman who has one glass of wine with lunch is considered to be operating under the influence. A 250 pound construction worker who has just one beer after work is under the influence.

The courts, lawyers, bondsmen, insurance companies and others all make money when someone has two beers and is charged with a DUI. At last estimate the national average cost of Driving Under the Influence is upwards of $15,000. That includes the attorney fees, bail-bond, increased insurance rates, lost wages, rehab, and the list goes on.

CHAPTER 20

EXTORTION
Threats to Withhold Funds

If some individual or corporation offered money to state lawmakers in exchange for passing a law utilizing the police powers of the state government, they would probably be charged with criminal bribery or extortion. Our federal bureaucrats are doing this very thing every day, and they are using a Trust Fund and taxpayers' money to do it.

Fraud and trickery is just as despicable when played by a government for "our own good" as it is when committed by a con-man or bunko-artist. In fact, when a con-man clips you for a few thousand, you can charge him with a crime and hopefully get some revenge or restitution. When a government agency tricks you into volunteering to give up one or more of your rights, they have deprived you of the very liberty they have sworn to protect and for which our nation is supposed to stand. When the courts become a willing participant in such chicanery, they are weakening the very foundations on which this nation was founded. It shouldn't be necessary for the general public to spend their waking hours trying to decide the differences between the rules, regulations and the laws…but we must!

Our government gets its authority to govern from the people. We, the people, cannot grant a power or authority we do not have. Common law says we may not take the property of another without payment or consent. That would be stealing. Our laws against theft do not exempt anyone. If a Congressman steals, he should go to jail. If a cop intentionally murders his wife, he should go to prison. The only time we can justify violating the rights of another is in preservation of our own rights. We can kill someone in self-defense or in defense of another. There are no exceptions to valid laws, but when we talk about rules and regulations there are exceptions all over the place. Our legislators are responsible for creating this system which bureaucrats then try to pawn off as actual laws. Many of those misleading regulations exempt the lawmakers.

Some people obey regulations even when they are obviously ridiculous. There is nothing wrong with obeying most rules, but you must be ready to cautiously disregard them when they are foolish, overly restrictive or require you to surrender any of your Rights.

Federal Speed Limit Trick Worked For a Decade!

The Congress' so-called national speed limit and the Federal Department of Transportation's (DOT) trickydictum that every state would have to pass 55 mph maximum speed laws or face penalties in the form of reduced highway funds was foisted on the 50 states starting in 1974 and was enforced for over 20 years. DOT took the position that the only purpose of the regulation was to conserve energy. At the time, the nation and the world was besieged with price manipulations by various oil producing nations.

The oil crisis, contrived or not, came at an ideal time for the DOT bureaucrats to cover their backsides. They blackmailed every state lawmaker into surrendering the police powers of their States and adopting 55 mph speed limits. It was either that or lose millions of dollars in highway trust funds - or so they thought.

The answer was really simple and could have been discovered by going back to *Square One* – requirements of any trust fund! To change the terms of any "trust fund" requires approval of all parties involved. Obviously the state legislators and governors had not knowingly agreed to change those terms - they were legally entitled to receive that money from the Highway Trust Fund! But they all forgot that they were only entitled to those funds at the "end of the designated year." If they wanted the money in advance, at the start of the year, they had to "voluntarily" apply for the funds and in doing so, agree to abide by the federal government's rule of having 55 mph speed limits.

I pointed this out to the new Arizona Governor Evan Mecham, who, in turn, presented it to the Western States Governor's Conference. It didn't take more than a few minutes for all those Governors to realize that they could thwart the Federal takeover of their traffic laws by not applying for the funds in advance. Two days later, the Federal government back-pedaled and repealed their demands about a 55 mph rule.

In fact, not one dollar of the money in the Trust Fund has been permanently withheld from any state. Sometimes there is a delay in sending the money to a state which is not considered to be complying with the various federal dictums, but eventually the money is paid. It would be illegal to alter the terms of the Trust without the consent of the beneficiaries of the Trust (the

states and the motorists who paid the taxes). Lawmakers should read the Trust Fund terms. It provides for
funding to be paid to the states at the end of the year. If
the state wants the money in advance the governor or
agent must apply for the funds and in doing so, agrees
to comply with all the "extra terms" in exchange for
getting the money in advance. At the end of the fiscal
year, the funds must be paid to the state.

Again, if a state has not been damaged (actually had
funds withheld in accordance with the terms of the Trust
Fund) all the threats of U.S. DOT mean nothing. If a
state goes to court "voluntarily" to challenge the implied threats, the courts can rule for what it considers
"public good" regarding that particular situation. Or, as
would most likely happen, the court would deny the
petition of the state and say that DOT had not done
anything illegal. Such a ruling is then erroneously construed to mean that DOT can "permanently" withhold
funds for failing to comply with certain DOT and other
agency rules; drinking age to 21, speed limits, emissions testing, seat belt regulations.

The problem with such broad interpretations being
put on the rules of procedure and law, is that even when
a lower court rules properly, that ruling can be appealed
until some higher court finally rules for "public good"
on the basis of *"Volenti Non Fit Injuria."*

When the machinery for the Highway Trust Fund was
put into place it was a binding trust agreement between
the states and the Federal government. The states would
collect a Federal gas tax at the pumps and send the
money to the Trust Fund. The Department of Transportation (DOT) administers the fund and appropriates the

money back to the states on the basis of need. It is a binding agreement and the Federal bureaucrats have no authority to withhold funds on the basis of rules they make later. Any threats to withhold funds are idle. The Administrators took the position that "if the states do not do as we dictate, then they obviously do not need the funds in advance."

Some state lawmakers protested, but were quickly shot down by the friends of the highway contractors and union leaders whose contracts and incomes depend on a constant flow of Highway Trust Fund dollars. Legislative lawyers, some well-versed in the voluntary trickery, discouraged the state legislators when they tried to fight back.

That trick, "withholding highway funds," continued for over 20 years and is still used in varying forms. It slipped by the scrutiny of some 200 State Governors, 200 Attorneys General, their staffs of lawyers and all the legislators who held office during that 20 year period. It is not always easy to see how the tricks are being played.

The same threats and tactics are being used to force all the states to have a "mandatory" seat belt rule or lose Highway Trust funds. Some states must check emissions of vehicles or lose Highway Trust funds.

Of course, these are all regulations, but you can see some of the problems you can encounter when you try to buck them. All of the rules are not bad. It is not the object of this book to make such a decision. You must do that for yourself — but only after you have been properly informed.

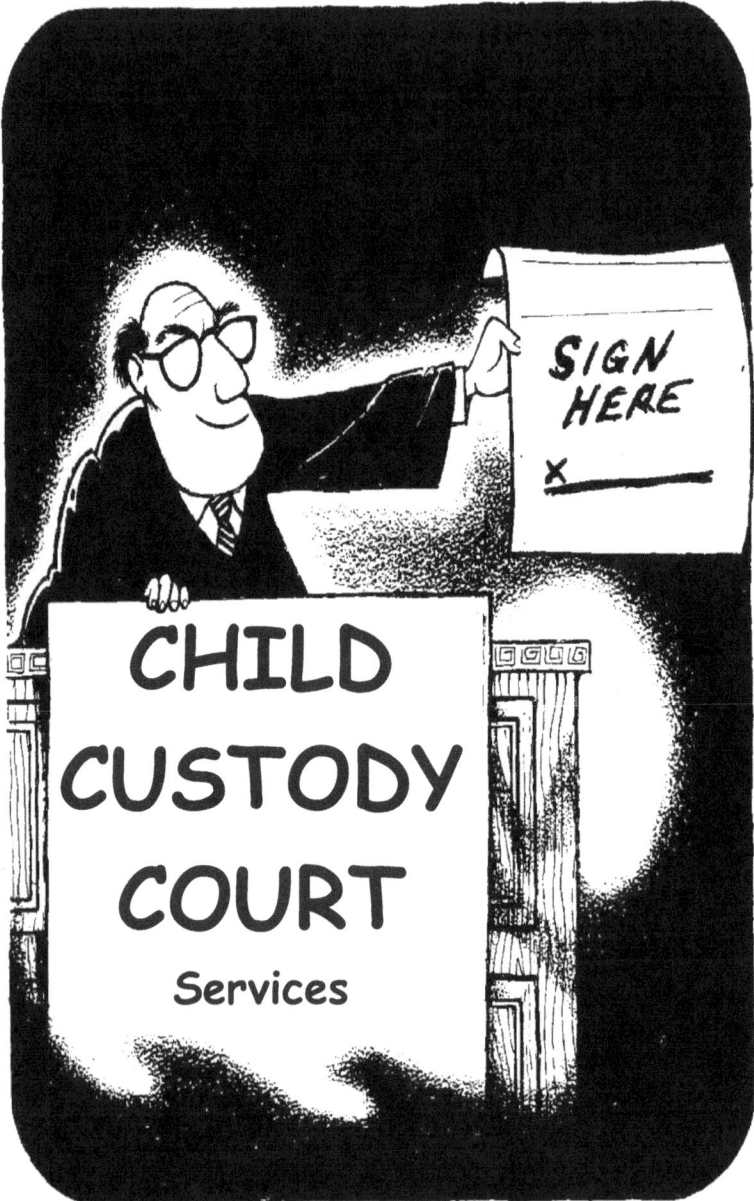

CHAPTER 21

CUSTODY
Your Child and the Courts

To some degree your children are your property, but not in the sense that you can do anything you please with them. They, too, have certain Unalienable Rights by virtue of their existence. But you, as a parent, have not only the responsibility for their well-being, but a right to take reasonable action to provide for their care, training and the direction of their life while they are minor children.

You can lose your rights over the care and custody of your children if you abuse them physically, refuse to educate them or fail to provide them with reasonable supervision or necessities of life - you can be charged with child neglect or abuse. If proven via due process of law, a court may declare the child a "Ward of the Court" and take over supervisorial duties and assign them to a child welfare agency or foster home.

There is another way you can lose custody of your children: Voluntary surrender! To voluntarily give up your legal or custodial rights over your children, you will have to enter into a domestic dispute (divorce action) in which the court is then given authority to determine which of the parents should have custody. There have been instances when the dispute was so bitter between the divorcing couple that the court refused to grant custody to either of the parents. Their Rights were not violated since they were in court voluntarily to have the terms of their marriage contract set aside. The only way to avoid this is to make certain you and the other parent come to a realistic agreement regarding child custody, support and visitation rights "before" your lawyers go in front of the judge. If you do not ask a direct question and give the judge a choice regarding custody, it is doubtful that the judge would try to assume such authority unless there is clear evidence that the child is in danger.

Children have been subjected to all manner of physical and sexual abuse in detention centers and even in court approved foster homes. The people who run such facilities are usually good people, but there are enough bad ones to fill several books with horror stories. Some children have even died in such facilities while concerned parents fought with juvenile court judges and child welfare workers to take their child out of the court's custody and return them to their home and family.

You must be proven unfit, the child is a danger to society or you volunteer your child for such a facility. If you are having problems with the child and seek counseling from some agency, they may suggest that such an incorrigible child might be better off if they were put into the "juvee" home (juvenile detention) for a while. To do this, you will usually have to sign papers granting the agency or a court the authority to take custody. You cannot rescind that permission or authority as easily as you can grant it. Once you grant jurisdiction over your child to that agency, you could have serious problems. Do not let anyone trap or trick you into voluntarily surrendering custody or authority over your child. Just because they have an official sounding title does not mean they know what is best. The fact that they work for the government might be reasonable cause for you to treat whatever advice they give you as suspect. Government believes it has a "compelling interest" in protecting minors from just about everything. Before "compelling government interests" can hold water, you have to agree or do harm to the child.

Do not sign any such authority or papers without your lawyer looking them over first. Do not be stampeded into doing anything just to temporarily "get your child out" of the detention center or court control.

Sometimes a child is taken to a youth detention center by the police if they are caught doing something illegal. That something "illegal" today might have been a "dumb thing" to do when you were a kid and nothing more than a "prank" in grandpa's day. But today it is considered a "criminal act" and the child is declared a "juvenile delinquent" just for pushing over an outhouse on Halloween.

It is important for any parent whose child is in custody for some offense to avoid making excuses and telling themselves that "My child wouldn't do that!" Half the time that is exactly what your child did - even gangster Al Capone's mother said her son wouldn't do the things the newspapers said he did.

Consider that leaving your son or daughter "locked-up" for a day might wake them up to the fact that they can get into serious trouble if they continue doing what they are doing. But it is essential that you show your concern by going to the place where your child is being held and making sure that they are healthy and let them know you love them and will do everything necessary to get them released - then wait a day or so - maybe even consult with an attorney if the matter is not just some prank that went astray.

Usually parents will be called by a child welfare officer to advise them that their child is in custody. Anxious parents usually make a beeline for the center to take the kid home. It is at this time you must be careful what you sign. You will always be asked to sign some document to get your child released. That document will usually be an agreement to "acknowledge authority of the state over your child" and you are merely being granted temporary custodial rights until the matter is resolved in court.

DO NOT SIGN SUCH AN AGREEMENT! Call your lawyer. Unless your child has actually been charged with a felony crime (murder, armed robbery, etc.), the juvenile authorities have only limited authority to detain him or her. If a serious crime is involved, often the agency will petition the court "ex-parte" - without notification to you. To hold a child who has not been charged with a crime, the agency must first go to a court of competent jurisdiction and petition for temporary custody until such time that a hearing is scheduled where they can try to prove you are an unfit parent. If you think you should be able to get a public defender under such circumstances, you can forget it in most states. Since a child custody action is not normally a criminal complaint, you will have to hire your own lawyer.

If you ever feel compelled to sign such a document without first getting informed advice of an attorney, do so only after you clearly print "Signed Under Duress" in the space just above where you will affix your signature. Horror stories abound regarding child protective services and when you fear for your child's safety, that is "duress." That will at least give a lawyer something to work with if you do hire one.

Do not let them turn the tables by tricking you into signing away your Rights or those of your minor child. They know how to apply the rules of procedure and when you are being intimidated regarding your child, chances are you will be inclined do whatever it takes – even if it is wrong!

JUST A REMINDER!

The power of the bureaucrats is great and they aren't going to surrender it easily. They will always find a new way to try and trick you. Remember: If you think it is wrong, it probably is — and you have to find out how the trick is being played!

MODIFIED FREEDOM

Legislative
Scribes

Limited Govt.

The
FOUNDING
FATHERS

DOLAN

CHAPTER 22

LEGISLATIVE SCRIBES
Wordsmith Spin-Masters

When the Supreme Court permits vagueness in the law and application of the rules as to give alternative choices for the meaning of words, they discredit all laws and make a mockery of justice. Our perception of the Constitution and our laws are constantly being manipulated and young college graduates have totally different views of their relationship and responsibility toward society and themselves than their parents and grandparents did.

Back door legislation has been going on at an excessive rate since 1954. For over 30 years Legislative Counsel for the U.S. Congress, Ward Hussey, headed a staff of lawyers who translated the desires of our elected Representatives in the House. He participated in the drafting of major legislation, including two versions of the Internal Revenue Code, the Marshall Plan, the Interstate Highway Act and Medicare. Today the office still exists and Sandra Lee Strokoff runs the show with the assistance of scores of young lawyers who "translate" the proposed legislation of Congressmen into the legal language of the U.S. Code (law) and subsequently the CFR (regulations). They do a great job of finding ways to circumvent the restrictions of the Constitution.

Most legislators seem to feel that as soon as they take

the oath to "uphold, protect and defend the Constitution," they have sworn an obligation to find ways to circumvent it!

State legislatures have similar law writers or scribes who try to rewrite all proposed laws in such a manner that they will not conflict with the state or U.S. Constitutions. Most are obviously good at it. They have written, legislators have passed, and the courts have upheld so much double-speak and gobbledygook that they have made it virtually impossible for most people to separate the voluntary rules, codes, regulation and ordinances from the real laws.

While doing some additional research for this book in Washington, DC, I had occasion to meet one of those retired "scribes. When I gave him a brief idea of what I intended to write he said, "Don't get carried away and rock the boat!" Can't imagine what he meant!

The lawyers and judges who know the distinct differences between these regulations and laws are doing a disservice to the people, the nation and liberty by concealing the information from the public. By permitting the people to be duped into believing that they are required to obey a rule or regulation as if it were a valid law, the door is open for the fascist controllers who would like to call a Constitutional Convention. They would attempt to amend or totally change our Constitution so that it conforms to the rules and regulations now being enforced. Then the rules will actually be laws!

Some time back a woman of means, and well educated, asked if I could give her daughter some pointers for a paper she was doing for a school assignment. Her subject: "How we get our rights from the government."

I pointed out to the woman that we don't get our rights from the government. We are the ones who created the government and gave certain restricted authority to it, and all other rights are ours by nature of our relationship to our creator and our fellow man. She seemed slightly shocked, but then replied, "That's certainly a novel concept!"

Novel Concept? It is the basis for our nation's existence, but people seem to forget - which came first, man or government? Obviously man created government! Government did not create man! Then government can only have those powers we already have and consent to give. In this nation, under our Constitution, we are supposed to be governed by consent of the governed. We are supposed to be a nation of laws, not of men. We have certain Unalienable Rights that cannot be denied except by due process of law (not rules) and no laws shall discriminate against anyone or be biased in favor of anyone.

If our leaders and lawmakers do not realize what is happening, then each day we will become more like the failed communist nations of the world, or worse — a socialist nation with compliance enforced by Nazi SS (without armbands); A land where a few people rule according to their own whims and the masses are workers or slaves. Whether the government usurps power and control via trickery and fraud to get the people to volunteer or they use guns, threats and even death to force their way to power and control, the end results will be the same.

CHAPTER 23

BE THE EXPERT
Resist: Pick Your Battles

If you want to be effective in fighting against bureaucratic controllers who try to usurp your Rights via intimidation and trickery, you must step out of the shadows and become somewhat of an expert. Then carefully pick and choose your own battle and the battleground. If you try to fight every regulation, procedure or rule, you will eventually be worn to a frazzle and defeated. To avoid such a defeat, you must opt to be a winner and that means you cannot play a sucker's game. You choose!

Obviously there are numerous injustices and battles to be fought. What is your area of expertise? Are you on solid ground to carry out the battle? Does your spouse and family support your efforts? Will your employer (source of income) understand what you are doing? Can you afford the fight — to win?

You must develop your expertise on some subject. You must be aware of exactly what you are doing if you decide to challenge the system in any area. Do not react in a knee-jerk fashion because you were unaware of the complexity of the situation. Plan your attack deliberately and carefully. You must know about the laws, regs and procedures relating to the arena of your battle. You cannot be expert on all the tactics and rules, so limit your fight to something you know. Become an expert by learning all about the particular subject and your opponents.

Can't do it? Of course you can! You are already an expert in some areas. You have been asked advice because someone felt you knew more about a subject than they did. That makes you an expert! An expert is someone who knows more than the other guys. Although many of your opponents declare themselves to be "experts", don't believe it! They just know a bit more than the average person and they play on it.

An example of how easy it is to be considered an expert on a subject came about when I wrote a simple 16-page booklet about how and why the U.S. was surrendering control of the Panama Canal. Panama is a "tax haven" nation and the President of Panama was threatening to change their laws and reveal the identities of all those wealthy foreigners who had accounts in his country. World leaders and many movie stars had money tucked away in Panama, out of sight of the tax collectors. President Jimmy Carter was inviting many of them into the White House, one at a time, to point this out, and invariably the big names would leave the Oval Office insisting that the Canal Zone should be given back to Panama. You might have pictured actor John Wayne leading a charge to keep the Canal, but he, too, left the President's office and insisted we had to surrender it to Panama.

That simple booklet was mailed out to over 1,000 embassies and governments around the world. As a result, the grandson of one of the primary engineers of the Panama Canal, wrote a letter to me asking that I come to address his group – because, as he described me, "you are an expert on the subject of the Panama Canal"! Expert? True, I had developed information others didn't consider, but that was all it took to be considered an "expert!" It doesn't take too much to be declared an expert!

When I organized cab drivers in El Paso, TX, I constantly fought with the city, police commissioner and the "expert" traffic engineer. Since I was not a "traffic engineer" it was an uphill battle - only to find out several years later that the expert traffic engineer's only experience was erecting stop signs in Phoenix, Az. So much for experts!

You must recognize that you are not alone in wanting to fight injustice. Others will also be fighting back. Give them your support whenever you can and resist whenever you can. Sometimes you can resist easily without creating a major battle for yourself. Ways in which you can easily resist include:

1 - Stop signing up for perks with all those companies that offer them in exchange for just a "little personal information". They are collecting data and sharing it with firms that will eventually use it to manipulate and control you.

2 - When someone asks you for personal information, especially your Social Security number, and it really is none of their business, politely tell them it is none of their business or give them transposed numbers (but not if it involves fraud).

3 - Give the information seekers false information to screw-up their data. But, NEVER give false information to a police officer — you can politely refuse to

give him certain information, but it is illegal to give him false information.

4 - If your job involves working for some controller corporation or the government and you see a way to help others by mis-filing data, consider doing it!

5 - If the person asking is the clerk at a store where you just made a cash purchase, give them all the false information you like – wrong phone, address, name - whatever. It will screw up their computer programming and might discourage such commercial information gathering in the future. However, a few states have laws that make it fraud to attempt to get a refund for products using false information.

The information seekers are almost immune to insults, so you should just appear to be polite and cooperative to really screw them up with incorrect information. Make sure that you don't give the name of another person who you know exists. That could be construed as impersonation, have further complications and in some states it could be construed as identity theft.

The system of rules the bureaucrats have created are exceptional and entangling. They have been at it a long time and many people have accepted it as a way of life.

Suppose you decide that the rule requiring vehicle emissions tests is invalid because it is discriminatory and exempts some vehicles. You refuse to have your car tested until the exceptions are removed. Now you try to pay your license tax and get the little tab for the current year. The bureaucrats might not let you have the license plate or tab until you comply with their unrelated rules, as mandated by U.S. DOT and EPA money. Frustrating, isn't it?

Be the expert! Go back another step (*Square One*). Why are you licensing your car? No, it is not a law! It is a rule. You must pay the tax on the vehicle — that is a valid law! The fact that you post your license on the car is just outward proof that the tax has been paid. The use of the license number for identification purposes is incidental to the tax being paid. You cannot be forced to surrender your right to move about in a safe manner in your own vehicle in exchange for proof of payment of a license fee and then have additional discriminatory rules made as a condition of using your vehicle. To force you to submit to such rules would violate your right to be treated equally. If the public health and safety necessitates emissions testing as the justification, then no vehicles can be exempt! If any vehicles are exempt, then it is a discriminatory regulation — not a law.

But your license plate is actually just a receipt to show you paid the tax on the vehicle. You can seal the receipt in plastic and paste it inside your rear window to make sure the entire world knows you paid the tax, but the local police officer might still pull you over to find out why you do not have a current license tab or plate. In this case, the cop becomes the buffer and you will most likely be cited and have to take your argument to the courts. Don't argue with the cop. If he is reasonable he will listen to your reasoning, but he will probably cite you anyway. Save your breath and the arguments for the courts!

Resisting such an established system is not going to be easy. You are better off fighting back now, while some of our Rights are still recognizable than to wait until our nation is completely converted to a totalitarian police state. Then the only way to fight back will be to put your life on the line.

Getting information out to others is a very effective way of fighting back and you can do it - as an expert! When you hear someone say anything to the effect that "we should have the right to...," point out to them that they already have that Right and they are confusing rules and regulations with actual laws and are voluntarily surrendering their Right.

You can write letters to the editor of the daily and weekly newspapers in your community, post your opinions on Facebook and other social media sites, Tweet or e-mail anyone who makes a statement that sounds like they have already surrendered. Contrary to what many people think, newspapers are seldom over-loaded with letters to publish. The editors love to get them and survey figures indicate that 25 percent of the dwindling subscribers read the letters to the editor regularly. Those are all great forums for expressing your views and making people aware of how they must protect freedom by challenging some of the control rules.

Utilize the social media whenever possible. You might reach just one concerned individual who could be the match to start a tremendous blaze for liberty and justice.

Speak up and let your views be known. I recall contacting some companies that were running TV ads and politely pointing out the errors in what the ads implied. Often, in as little as two-weeks, the ads were pulled or changed. Speak up - someone might listen!

No matter how religious or irreligious you might be, avoid bringing religion into any battles to correct what is happening. Pro or con on any religious subject is a personal opinion and unlikely to influence most businesses, the government or people of another faith.

You have adversaries and to be effective in resisting the bureaucrat controllers, you must clearly idenfity the real culprits - your enemies! They are out there and they will try to thwart your good efforts. Be prepared!

Yes - You Can Speak!

Do your knees shake when you get up to speak? Sit on the side and watch the knees of the so-called experts when they stand up to talk. That podium is there to give them something to lean on and hide their shaking knees. If you find you are reluctant to speak out or challenge the so-called experts at public meetings, consider taking a Dale Carnegie Course in public speaking or join your local Toastmasters club.

Everyone is nervous when they first start to talk to a large number of people. Even small groups can make someone nervous. You can learn how to overcome such fears by taking a speaking course. Your local community college offers such courses and you can learn a lot and get practical experience by joining your local Toastmasters — you will benefit greatly from meeting the people as well as the experience you will get speaking in public.

CHAPTER 24

MORALITY AS LAW!
Whose Morality Would You Accept As Law?

While many good people demand legislation regarding "morality" and want to make it illegal to engage in any conduct or activity which they deem sinful or immoral, they rush to defend "their Rights" to Freedom of Religion according to the First Amendment!

What would happen to our society if we adopted as LAWS some of the primary beliefs of every religion? Could we live?

Under Catholicism, nobody could be divorced and remarried. Ditto for Judaism and many other faiths. Such actions are immoral and sinful.

If the Mormons could make the laws for everyone, all alcoholic beverages would be immoral and outlawed.

Jehovah's Witnesses would have a law against blood transfusions.

Some Baptists and other preachers would have a law against dancing - immoral - leads to sex.

Pentecostals would make it illegal for anyone to wear jewelry and it would be against the law (sinful equals illegal) to wear make-up.

The Amish would ban all TV, radios, telephones, autos, airplanes and computers - immoral - because these things make weak people out of us all. They would also make education beyond an 8th grade level illegal.

Christian Science would make medical doctors illegal - medicines, too would be against the law.

It would be a law that every male would be circumcised - and some religions would even require that of women. Some religions would require the women to cover their legs to the ankles or be branded immoral - and others would have morality laws passed requiring all women to have their faces veiled. All men would have to allow their facial hair to grow or they would be immoral.

Islam would prohibit money lending for profit and require a death penalty for an adulteress - immoral. The Islamic faith also considers use of force (jihad), including outright murder, a "moral act" when conducted for the purpose of bringing non-believers or heretics to accept their religion.

Nobody would be allowed to have statues of religious figures - Pork would be illegal and nobody would be allowed to kill a steer.

Of course, most would make it a morality law to smoke a cigarette, appear nude before consenting adults, have sex with someone to whom you are not married (by each religion's doctrine). Some would make it illegal to have any sex except for the purpose of procreation - and that would have to be missionary style - and with clothes on.

Nobody could conduct any form of business on Saturday and Sunday - or even do their own chores.

Abortions? That would be considered murder, regardless of circumstance - even if it meant the mother would have to die!

Music? That, too, would be illegal - all types! Buddhists would... you get the picture?

MORALITY??????? Whose Morality?????

In these United States we are supposed to have laws within the limitations (limited government) written down as our Constitution. But some people, including our lawmakers and judges, seem to think "We the People..." created our government to tell us what our "Moral Standards" should be.

If we are to accept any of these "morality" positions and pass it as a law, then we must adopt the moral beliefs, dogma, doctrines and tenets of all religions.

Who would be willing to have ALL of the above mentioned "Morality Standards" passed as LAWS? Remember, you don't get to pick and choose — ALL as LAWS or NONE!

THIS SHOULD BE THE ONLY MORAL STANDARD: People are free to do as they please unless they cause actual harm to another. If harm is caused, the injured party (or government acting on the injured party's behalf) should take action - make a specific charge, prove the damage to the person injured, and allow the accused to face their accuser.

Laws are written to "protect" the people and their rights. Regulations are written to "control" the people and almost always limit their rights.

You Can't Dig Him Up To Apologize!

CHAPTER 25

DEATH "PENALTY!"

Who Gave Government That Authority?

You, as an individual, do not have the right to kill another human being except as a matter of self-defense (or defense of another). Do you agree?

While the debates go on about the right and wrong of using a death sentence as a punishment, few, if any, go back to *Square One* to justify their dissertations. Authors like Bill Kurtis (*The Death Penalty on Trial*) and others point out the numbers of innocent people who have been sentenced to death row and even executed. A historical and theological look at the subject by James J. Megivern (*The Death Penalty*) puts emphasis on the biblical "eye for an eye" and religious justifications as he questions the moral right to have the state take the life of another human being.

Although most debates on the subject go way back in history, none looks at the basic foundations of the United States of America – the Declaration of Independence and the phrase "Unalienable right to life …" The prefix UN is the key! That prefix means NOT! Your right to life cannot be taken away except as a matter of self-defense. That is the only authority the people have ever had and the government cannot presume to have an authority the people could not grant to the government!

Since the government, at all levels, was created by

the people and receives its authority from the people, it raises the question - "Where did government get the authority to authorize a death 'penalty' sentence to anyone - except in defense of society?" If we, as individuals, cannot take revenge or penalize someone by killing them, where did government get that authority?

Government can execute (kill) a person if it is determined that the person would most likely murder another individual if given the chance. If a person commits murder for hire it is reasonable to assume they would do so again - if the price was right. That individual should be executed as a matter of "self-defense" of society. Sending such a person to prison would subject every person in prison, including the guards, to the possibility of being murdered by that convicted killer! It is human nature to want "revenge" for the murder of a loved one, but keeping our human nature in check is what civility, valid law and justice is all about.

Each time the U.S. Supreme Court considers a "death penalty" case, the Justices fail to consider the word "penalty" or the presumed authority of anyone to penalize another via execution - killing them. We put people in prison (restrict their liberty) as a means of defending society and the same is true of restricting their pursuit of happiness - and all such restrictions on "unalienable rights" are self defense to protect society from the aggressor for a reasonable period of time. Hopefully, while in prison, the incarcerated person will learn to respect the rights of others or become too old to violate the rights of others.

There are many other arguments against government executing a person, not the least of which is the fact that no judge, jury or witness is infallible - they make mistakes! When someone is executed, the mistake cannot be corrected. Society cannot apologize to a dead person and make things right!

Another point in the "protection of society" is consideration of a claim that a killer is of diminished capacity - insane or under a certain age. What difference does it make to the dead victims if the killer with an IQ of 40 doesn't and will never know that killing someone is wrong? What difference does it make to innocent people who may be the next victim of an individual who is insane? Society has a right to defend itself from such a person and, depending on the circumstances, has the authority to execute such a killer!

"The only justification for taking the life of anyone is "self-defense" and that includes the defense of another! That is the only authority "we, the people" have ever had and that is the only authority we could ever give to our government!"

Jay Evenson

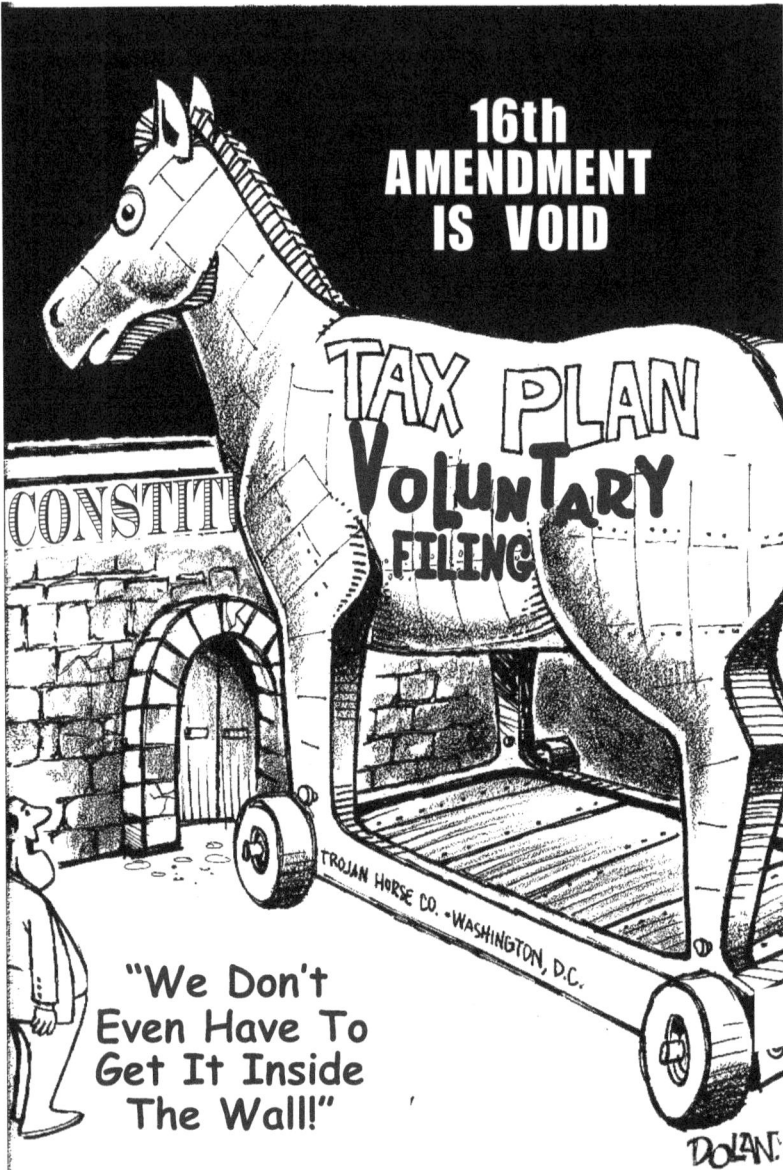

16th
AMENDMENT
IS VOID

TAX PLAN
VOLUNTARY
FILING

CONSTIT

TROJAN HORSE CO. •WASHINGTON, D.C.

"We Don't
Even Have To
Get It Inside
The Wall!"

DOLAN

CHAPTER 26

THAT 16th AMENDMENT
Personal Income Tax Trick

There is always someone or some organization claiming that the Personal Income Tax procedures are not authorized by law. That is, the 16th Amendment to the U.S. Constitution was not ratified and therefore the Federal government has no authority to levy a tax on most individuals. While the 16th Amendment continues to be printed and appears to exist, Congress actually negated it as related to income tax with the Public Law 97-248, 1982, an act of Congress.

It is not the purpose of this book to tell anyone whether or not they should "volunteer" to continue filing personal income tax forms. The purpose of the following information is so each can individually make that "informed" decision for themselves and if they choose to volunteer - do it!

A book entitled *"The Law That Never Was"* by Bill Benson and Martin "Red" Beckman (1985) is still in print today. It points out that the 16th Amendment (Direct Taxation) was not ratified "by the legislatures" of the required number of states as required in the U.S. Constitution. For over 70 years the basis of authority for most of the Internal Revenue Code was predicated on that un-ratified amendment for direct taxation.

The two men had been testifying in Federal Court in

a tax trial. Beckman had copies of the various legislative acts that had been passed by State legislatures between 1909 and 1913 that related to the proposed 16th Amendment. The documents proved that the 16th Amendment was NOT ratified by the required number of "state legislatures". But the judge refused to accept the documents as evidence because they were not certified by the Secretaries of State for each state.

The men and their wives decided to travel to each state and collect "certified copies" of the documents. But, in the meantime, skull-duggery was underway. The revelations of Beckman and Benson put the federal government in a bind and it now had to find a way to trick the people into filing and paying taxes without the legal authority of the non-ratified 16th Amendment. If it returned to the original process of billing each state for its share of federal expenditures the financiers and bureaucracy would be in shambles. How could they ma-

---

TO CATCH A THIEF

A con-man or bunko scammer has two choices in adopting a method of operation: (1) Keep it Simple. (2) Make it complicated and extensive.

When governments wants to circumvent restrictions it generally follows both of the rules for being a thief. The bureaucrat-controllers adopt a simple plan and inter-mix an inconspicuous word or phrase that is a revelation of how it works. Then they proceed to complicate the structure with numerous rules, regulations, decrees, policies and programs to frustrate even the most avid researchers in search of the truth. To catch a thief you must go back to *Square One!*

NOTICE: If you have not read the first part of this book, there is a good chance that you do not completely understand that "volunteering" makes you subject to the rules and regulations, just as if they are valid laws. Be sure you know what it means to volunteer so that you will understand how this personal income tax trick is being played.

nipulate and control the States if they couldn't entice or bribe them with federal funding? How would they collect the money to pay the interest on all the money they borrowed - the National Debt? It has been calculated by numerous financial experts that the total of all current personal income tax revenues barely pays the interest and maintenance costs of that every growing National Debt.

As a result of reading that book and then doing research to prove or disprove the claims, it didn't take much to discover that in 1982, the 94th Congress amended *Public Law (97-248)* and repealed Subtitle A of the Internal Revenue Code. That subtitle encompassed all of the "laws" relating to personal income tax and specifically states that all application and administration of subtitle A of the Internal Revenue Code of 1954 and any amendments thereto shall be carried out as if the Act had not been enacted. Since Subtitle A was also based on the Internal Revenue Code of 1939, that was also repealed and the "authority presumed" as a result of the 16th Amendment, as referenced, was no longer necessary for the application of the direct taxation policies of the Internal Revenue Code. To make sure that everyone would be mislead and look no further, there were references to *Title 18 – Criminal Code* and other Codes. Each time the reference stated "see" such and such. But in several areas of the codes, including Subtitle D of the code (*7806*), it states, regarding cross references, that where the word "see" is used, it is for convenience, and "shall have no legal effect".

As for General Jurisdiction of the courts, in *IRS Code - 7402*: "For general jurisdiction of the district courts of the United States in civil actions involving internal revenue, see section 1340 of title 28 of the United States Code." There's that word again – "see". It can be found throughout the newly revised internal revenue code.

Since the 16th Amendment no longer gave the federal government legal authority for collecting direct taxes from the citizens they had to find a way of tricking the people into voluntarily filing tax forms. Since the public had been filing every year for so many years, the scribes and tricksters determined they could really have "The world's greatest voluntary tax filing system." All that was necessary is to stop talking about the authority they didn't have, pass some extremely convoluted regulations and the people would never know. They would continue to file. Once a person has "voluntarily" signed the form 1040, they were volunteering for the entire system. The final numbers on the tax return was the amount they "volunteered" to pay and the IRS could continue collecting as they had in the past. New Regulations would have to be adopted and procedures changed.

A lot of bases had to be covered so that people like Bill Benson and Martin "Red" Beckman, Irwin Schiff and dozens of other tax protestors could not readily find out how the trick was being played. Although the two men were correct in the book they eventually wrote, *"The Law That Never Was"*, Beckman and Benson were scratching their heads when, after collecting all those certified copies, the federal judge declared the non-ratification of the 16th Amendment "moot!" What they did not realize was that some deceptive changes had already been made by the upper echelon and the government could now just trick the people into "volunteering to file" and then be required to pay direct taxes. As recently as 2008 a federal court stated that the documentation of non-ratification Mr. Benson was referencing in seminars was "irrelevant." The IRS no longer needed that so-called 16th Amendment in order to collect the reported taxes.

One of the changes in the newer IRS Codes includes a regulation that prohibits the agency and its agents from referring to tax protestors as "illegal tax protestors"! *(Subtitle H, Sec. 3707. Illegal tax protester designation)*.

Did Congress Know?

Some members of Congress (Senate and House) had to know, but many were just fooled by the legislative scribes or weren't paying attention. Eventually the scribes got around to reviewing a booklet authorized by the 95th Congress in 1977 – ***The Constitution Of The United States Of America*** *(House Document No. 95-256)*. It included the original Constitution, all the amendments, and a synopsis of the ratification certification, Analytical Index and the proposed but unratified amendments. That little booklet could be a trouble maker and in order to mislead the people it would be necessary to make a couple of subtle changes, without drawing attention. Congress published the booklet again in 1986 (*House Document No. 100-94*) with the two seemingly minor alterations.

THOSE REVEALING BOOKLETS!

THE FIRST BOOKLET (1976) with a charcoal grey cover printed each amendment with a commentary:

"It was declared in a proclamation *(sometimes a certificate)* by the Secretary of State dated *xxxxxx*, to have been ratified by the legislatures of *XX* of the *XX* States."

That is what is required by the U.S. Constitution – it must be ratified by the **legislatures**! The other means of ratification authorized is that it be done by the States in **Convention** and that was only done once with the 21st Amendment *(repeal of the 18th – Prohibition)*. That certification was:

"It was declared, in a certificate of the Acting Secretary of State, dated December 5, 1933, to have been **ratified by conventions** in 36 of the 48 States." A correct means of ratification.

But when it came to the 16th Amendment, the commentary stated:

"It was declared, in a proclamation of the Secretary of State, dated February 25, 1913, to have been **ratified by 36 of the 48 States.**" But the Constitution requires that it be ratified by the "legislatures of the States" – not just the governor or someone representing the State. That one glaring bit of print could unravel everything as the controllers attempted to deceive the people.

THE SECOND BOOKLET (1986) had a much fancier cover *(House Document No. 100-94)* but the pages were virtually the same – except for changes to the commentary under the 21st Amendment: the certification omitted the words "conventions in" and just stated, like the 16th, that it had been "ratified by 36 of the 48 States." Now the glaring omission of "legislatures" won't be so noticeable!

All other amendments were certified to have been ratified by the legislatures of the States.

Numerous new tax regulations were adopted and old ones amended to avoid a possible reference to the 16th Amendment. The scribes were kept busy and by 1995 there were over 40,000 pages of tax regulations as opposed to fewer than 3,000 pages of Title 26 in 1981. By the start of 2014 the codes had been virtually rewritten and totaled over 74,000 pages of double-speak codes and regulations.

It is interesting to note that the combined holy books of 4 religions – Judaism, Islam, Christianity – plus the Book of Mormon - define and promulgate their beliefs, history, rules and decrees in a combined total of less than 4,000 printed (English language) pages. In that paltry number of pages, almost half the civilized world attempts to define God, Allah, Jehovah, the planet earth, the heavens and the nature of man. Many of those religious books use very small type, so assume you use very large type (for the old folks) – maybe 8,000 pages!

But the IRS code now has over 74,000 printed pages to define the tax structure of the United States of America! If they want to keep the scam going, they have to make it complicated!

Can You Just Stop Filing A Tax Return?

If you have been unknowingly filing a "voluntarily"

tax return, you could have some expensive problems if you just stop filing. When you filed you were given certain perks (deductions, offsets and delays) to reward you for prompt volunteering and payment of the amounts you stated you owed. Those perks can easily be construed to be "unearned" if you don't continue to file in good faith. As a result, in civil matters, the IRS can go back three years to audit your returns (and further back if you filed amended returns). If they find any attempt to defraud the government (income you didn't declare on the forms you filed) you could be charged with "willful" criminal fraud – for that they can usually go back 7 years.

Although Congress repealed Subtitle A of the code in 1980, the act required that it be enforced "as if it never existed." That means it must still be printed and made available (how else could you enforce it as if it never existed unless you know what once existed?). But they did not cancel Sub-Titles B through D, and these can be the trap that ensnares you.

One provision of the remaining subtitles is that "All taxes are due at the source." If you are employed and your boss or his accountant believes the money they pay you is subject to income tax, they will have to pay it unless you file a W-2 form allowing the employer to withhold that money from your check. This makes it tough on anyone who works for or operates as a corporation, LLC or some other designation created with permission of the government. If you are self-employed as an individual you can make the decision to file and pay – or drop-out!

Remember – you "volunteer" to file those returns and

once you acknowledge that you owe the money – you owe it! Filing is voluntary and there is no tax due unless you file. Once filed, you owe the money! Because most filers have taken numerous deductions over the years, the IRS (those responsible to collect money you said you owe) knows where most of your assets are located.

A key term in any prosecution of "failure to file" is the word "willful". If you do not believe you are required to file any form with the government, not filing is NOT a "willful act". If, however, you believe you are required to do something like file a tax return and you refuse, neglect or fail to do it, that is a "willful act" and may be subject to prosecution.

Your state may have an income tax system - that is a legal tax. But if the state adjusts the filing based on the IRS Codes and procedures, it may not be compulsory that you file a return with the state unless you volunteer for the IRS process. But even the state tax structure is on thin ice since they are constitutionally prohibited from making anything but gold or silver coin legal tender in payment of a debt. *(See Chapter 29).*

It isn't likely that most people will stop filing and paying personal income taxes just because they know the 16th Amendment was not ratified. Most will take the line most familiar to them, just as the citizens did in Nazi Germany – they just go along!

Filing a 1040
or other Income Tax Report Is "Voluntary" - but once you sign it and file it, you have agreed to pay all the taxes indicated on the form - and to comply with all the government regulations related to it!

BEWARE: THE END RESULT

Most likely we will see a concerted push for a Constitutional Convention to stop government encroaching on our Rights, but the people who will be designated to change our Constitution won't necessarily do what we want. The changes would most likely be those that would cause it to conform to the procedures and rules presently being used by government. When one of the delegates to the Convention argues against taking private property for Public Good and turning it over to a private developer, he or she will be soundly admonished and told, "We've been doing it for years!"

When calls for a change to the Constitution originate with an elected official (unless such an amendment further restricts government or expands individual reserved rights) the official is in violation of his or her oath to "protect and defend" the Constitution.

When a Constitutional Convention is called, those selected delegates from each state can change it in any manner they choose. Who do you trust?

What happens will be up to you — YOU! Not George or your kids or your parents or your teacher or your government. It is up to YOU!

PART TWO

STATUE of LIBERTY
Redesigned by
Republicans and Democrats!

DOLAN

CHAPTER 27

JUST FIX IT!
Make It So-

Part One of this book explained how the government and major corporations play their dirty tricks. Part Two presents some solid ideas and programs to change, adjust and amend the laws and procedural systems now being used to control all the people.

There are some drawbacks to advocating for change. I learned of three back when Gerald Ford became our first "un-elected" President. The economy was in a state of disarray and the unemployment rate was in excess of 9 percent. President Ford started pushing "WIN" buttons and flags to try and induce companies to hire more people. It wasn't working!

My income was fairly good at the time and I decided to promote an idea that would create a real incentive to companies, big and small, to hire more workers. Flying to Washington, DC, I planned to spend a couple of weeks and several thousand dollars to promote the plan. I collared several different Congressmen and a couple of Senators and they all seemed to like the idea. Each referred me to another of their fellow legislators. And each, without exception, asked the same question: "How long are you planning to be in town?"

Naïve as I was, I didn't realize the significance of their questions. At the time I assumed members of congress wanted to solve the nation's problems. Hah! They just wanted to know how long they would have to be polite and put up with me.

During my three weeks in the nation's capital, I ran ads in many of the newspapers the legislators and their staffs would most certainly read such as *Roll Call* and the *Washington Times* (I couldn't afford the *Washington Post*). After 20 days of pitching the idea I could see that it wasn't getting any real support from anyone and, slightly discouraged, I boarded a flight to return home. On board I sat next to a well-dressed man and we engaged in some polite conversation about D.C. and what goes on there.

He asked what I had been doing and I explained the idea to him (never know who you're sitting next to on a plane - could have been someone with some influence). After explaining it in detail about how it would put people back to work and develop the economy, he asked, "What's in it for you? How do you make out if they do this?"

Again, my naïveté was on display. "Nothing." I commented. "I just want to see the nation and the economy get moving."

A few seconds later the gentleman excused himself, got up from his seat and walked toward the back of the aircraft. Sure enough, he had taken a seat in another section of the plane. I had to think, "Did I take a shower that morning?" Checked the armpits and recalled I had taken a shower - and my shoes were still on my feet, so I knew that smell couldn't be what drove him away." It had to be my statement that I was spending all this time and money for public good and there was nothing in it for me, personally!

Over these many years I learned a number of lessons about society, politics and government - and how things work:

1 – After they are elected, most politicians just give lip service to issues and they only do that if it will help them get re-elected and remain in power.

2 - Career bureaucrats and lobbyists actually control most of what goes on in Washington, DC.

3 – Most people don't really care too much about an issue until it is their turn in the "screw the people" barrel. Then they are ready to act!

The Constitution should never be changed or amended for slight and transient cause. But when the shortcomings of that revered document become obvious and have been twisted and circumvented to cause the denial of Rights and create corruption in our system for over 100 years the causes are not transient and amendments and changes must be made.

CHAPTER 28

CHANGES ARE NEEDED
The Way It Was and Should Be!

When our nation was created as a Republic it utilized Democratic procedures to elect the people who would run the country. It was done with much concern about combining independent commonwealths and sovereign states into a "united" group of states. Over the past 200 years that has changed dramatically

The original plan was that the states would control the federal government. The people would elect their Congressional Representatives (based on population). They were elected for 2 years and the people could throw them out if they didn't like what they were doing. U.S. Senators were elected by the state legislatures. If the state legislators felt their delegate to the U.S. Senate was not acting in a manner that served the best interests of their state, they could recall that Senator and the state legislators could conduct a hearing and, if they chose, designate (elect) another person to be the U.S. Senator from their state. Although that didn't happen and most U.S. Senators remained in their position for the full six years, the threat of a recall by their respective state legislatures kept those Senators in line.

The theory was that the people of each state could easily contact their state legislator since he (or she) lived within a few miles and often worked in the area. The legislator was also more likely to be working on behalf of the state and could keep an eye on what the U.S. Senator was doing – and without much fanfare could recall that person and replace their U.S. Senator.

The cost of operating the Federal government was in the hands of the U.S. Congress which was given the authority to originate the spending of the people's money. Whatever budget (expense) Congress adopted was then divided by the Census Bureau's population figures and a bill was sent to each sovereign member-State. Each state could then collect their share of those taxes for the operations of the Federal government by whatever means the state legislature deemed appropriate – property taxes, income taxes, corporate taxes, sales taxes of any other fees or taxes they chose. If the people didn't like the way the taxes were levied in their particular state they could elect a different state legislator or governor to office – or they could move to some other state where they liked the tax system employed.

This method of financing the Federal government's expenditures kept the spending in check for over 100 years. There was no National Debt to be passed on to future generations – it was "pay as you go" or "you go away quickly."

The 16th Amendment to authorize direct taxation on the citizens (income tax) was sent to the states but the federal government started operating on the presumption (and deceit) that it had been ratified by the required number of state legislatures when it had not been legally ratified.

The 17th Amendment to the U.S. Constitution allowing the people to directly elect their U.S. Senators was passed just a few years later. Those Senators were now free from state controls and could run amuck, if they chose, and the voters won't even know what is happening. They are now the elitists who can do pretty much as they please for five years – and during the final year before they face the voters again, they start working on double-talking the people of their state to re-elect them.

The states are supposed to control the Federal government – not the other way around. As long as the governors and state legislators have no control over how to collect the money the federal government spends and no control over any branch of national government, the autocracy of the federal government will continue, the national debt will keep increasing, foreign governments and banks will own or control our nation and "We, the people..." will become nothing more than a historic expression of days gone by!

1 - Repeal the publication and application of the 16th Amendment by having the President or the Secretary of State file a **"Certificate of Erratum"** in that the previous certification of ratification was improvidently made.

Why Not Just Repeal It?

A certificate of erratum is a legal term that is usually used as a correction of a printing, typographical, or editorial error. The term is often used in the Latin formula for the assignment of mistakes made in a court case. Erratum is also a correction of a book or article. An erratum is most commonly issued shortly after its original text is published, but may be used anytime!

Officially filing such a certification would be far less of a problem than filing an amendment to repeal a non-amendment. Primary concern on repealing something that doesn't exist is that failure of the required number of state legislatures to do so could be construed that they were, in fact, ratifying the 16th Amendment. You can bet the insider bureaucrats and controllers in Washington would support such a repeal amendment - another trick they would like play!

When everyone knows that they are not required to pay homage to the IRS codes and demands, there will be problems for the states and the federal government. Washington will have to follow the constitutional mandates and resort to sending bills to each State for the proportionate costs of federal expenses and each state will have to consider how it wants to collect the money.

However, troublesome as that might be, it would stop Washington from running up the National Debt - the States would not allow it!

2 - Repeal the 17ᵗʰ Amendment and restore the United States Senate to the control of the State legislatures as was originally designed by the founding fathers when they drafted and adopted the Constitution.

Let The States Control Washington!

Many public figures have been critical of the 17th Amendment - direct election of U.S. Senators by the voters instead of the State legislatures. One critic was Senator Zell Miller of Georgia as he announced his retirement in 2004. He called for a repeal of the 17th Amendment.

Senator Miller pointed out that direct elections had allowed Washington's special interests to "call the shots, whether it is filling judicial appointments or issuing regulations. The state governments aided in their own collective suicide by going along with the popular fad of the time."

According to those who advocate for repeal of the 17th Amendment, Congress would not have been able to pass so many unfunded mandates if the Senators were still selected by and answerable to their respective State legislatures.

Voters can reach their elected state representatives, but trying to directly speak to a U.S. Senator is almost as difficult as directly speaking to the President of the United States.

3 - Adopt an amendment regarding Transparency of Court Certiorari (Review) Rulings -

Whenever the high court is petitioned for a review it has a choice to accept the petition and consider it or ignore the petition and let the lower court's ruling prevail. The Justices of the Supreme Court rarely state their reasons for refusing to consider an issue presented to them. They rely on the fact that they have already answered the question in some distant previous ruling by the Court.

While that procedure (or lack of it) may satisfy the requirements of the U.S. Constitution, it creates confusion in the minds of the media, most attorneys and the public. It distorts justice!

If the highest court of the land is interested in true "Justice For All" it must clarify its reasons for allowing a lower court ruling to stand. They must be specific or they are not maintaining the spirit of the Constitution.

LEGAL TRANSPARENCY AMENDMENT
ARTICLE _____

Section 1- The Supreme Court of the United States, and all lower courts, are required to clearly state in writing, not just by reference, the specific reasons for granting or denying review of each and every petition to said Court.

Section 2 - The Court will state, at the outset of any finding or ruling, the specific legal precedents, Stare Decisis basis and legal maxims applied in any and all majority decisions.

Section 3 - Failure to comply with the spirit of this provision will be prima facia evidence of grounds for impeachment of each and every Justice that is a signatory to the Majority findings.

4- Adopt a Limited Treaties Amendment

Everyone makes mistakes and our founding fathers were no exception. The seemingly harmless provision about authority to enter into "treaties" with foreign powers is being used to destroy America as we know it! Treaties virtually nullify every State constitution and the U.S. Constitution.

Every so-called Free Trade Agreement (FTA) creates "courts" that cannot be over-ruled by any U.S. court – including the Supreme Court of the United States. All foreign businesses involved in U.S. operations under a FTA (treaty) are virtually exempt from U.S. and state laws, rules, regulations, controls and taxes. Small businesses, farmers and property owners cannot compete when they have to obey the law and the FTA firms are exempt.

Without this amendment, the controllers in Washington can continue to "sign-away" the protections and limits of the entire U.S. and every State constitution.

LIMITED TREATIES AMENDMENT
ARTICLE _____

Sect. 1 -No Treaty, agreement or provisions thereof, made or entered into by any act of any branch of government, agency or official, shall diminish, set aside, restrain or relinquish the authority or rights provided or reserved in this Constitution, of any branch of government, any court, any state, any enterprise or any individual.

Sect. 2 – This Amendment limits provisions and authority of the words "Treaty" or "Treaties" as used in ARTICLES 1, 2, 3 and 6 of The Constitution Of The United States. The U.S and State Constitutions shall withstand any treaty.

5 - Support State ratification of this Amendment to reserve constitutionally enumerated Rights to the People, not corporations. U.S. Senator Bernie Sanders (I) has sponsored an amendment that is currently working its way thru the U.S. Senate.

ALTERNATE STATE OPTION: Until Senator Sanders' amendment is approved and ratified, each State can take immediate action to defuse the corporate buying of elections. Corporations exist because some state allowed them to be created - and they are not registered voters - corporations cannot vote! Adopting simple state laws that prohibit anyone from contributing to or in any way influencing the election of candidates or issues unless they are a "Registered Voter" within the state will crimp the buying of elections!

"Saving American Democracy Amendment."
ARTICLE_____

"SECTION 1. The rights protected by the Constitution of the United States are the rights of natural persons and do not extend to for-profit corporations, limited liability companies, or other private entities established for business purposes or to promote business interests under the laws of any state, the United States, or any foreign state.

"SECTION 2. Such corporate and other private entities established under law are subject to regulation by the people through the legislative process so long as such regulations are consistent with the powers of Congress and the States and do not limit the freedom of the press.

"SECTION 3. Such corporate and other private entities shall be prohibited from making contributions or expenditures in any election of any candidate for public office or the vote upon any ballot measure submitted to the people.

"SECTION 4. Congress and the States shall have the power to regulate and set limits on all election contributions and expenditures, including a candidate's own spending, and to authorize the establishment of political committees to receive, spend, and publicly disclose the sources of those contributions and expenditures.".

6 - Adopt legislation that stops the Federal Reserve System's authorization to accept anything except the U.S. Treasury's bonds or securities as authorization to print or issue monetary credits.

The original establishment of the Federal Reserve (FED) seemed like a reasonable idea at the time - A Central Bank! But it has gone far beyond the original intent and is now the tool of irresponsible member banks, financial institutions and corrupt individuals in the U.S. and around the world..

The Banking Act of 1933 was a law that introduced banking reforms to control speculation by banks and other investors that led to the stock market collapse and the Great Depression. It was commonly called the *Glass-Steagall Act* and remained in effect until Congress repealed it with the *Depository Institutions Deregulation and Monetary Control Act of 1980*. That act also allowed the FED to invest in "private bonds" and eventually to invest in the bonds of foreign banks

Long story short, repeal of the Glass-Steagall Act and subsequent acts of Congress effectively removed separations between investment banking securities and commercial banks. This, in turn, led to the financial debacle of 2007 when the prevailing attitude was that the banks were "to big to fail", resulting in using public funds for TARP to bail them out!

To fix this problem it is essential that the Glass-Steagall Act be revived, putting banks and the Federal Reserve System in check.

If outside sources are ever privy to the real Federal Reserve' books and are allowed to audit them, the FED will crumble.

7- Amend Articles 8 and 10 that authorize Congress to establish weights and measures, including gold and silver coin value. Add the words following "has the Power" - "<u>and is required</u>" to establish the value thereof.

When the founding fathers adopted the Constitution and "gave power" to Congress to regulate the value of gold and silver coin as related to any currency issued, they could not have conceived of a process that would allow creation of money with absolutely nothing to back it up. They expected the States to keep the Federal government's money presses in check.

We must return to a monetary standard of some type and throughout history gold and silver has been the anchor!

CHAPTER 29

GOLD & SILVER
Force States To Adhere To Constitution

Shortly after this nation was formed as the United States of America, Congress adopted a bi-metal standard using gold and silver. They set the nation's fledgling currency at $19.30 a troy ounce and proceeded to order coinage based on that standard. They understood that without a standard of measurement it would be like going into the butcher shop and not knowing how much ground beef was in a pound. Fixed standards are essential to a level economic playing field. A large segment of U.S. society and many foreign nations would like to see a return to a gold standard – or any standard that would allow commerce without inflation.

The free-spending government will not do it, but the people can by putting pressure on their respective state governments. The U.S. Constitution *(Article I, Sect. 10)* specifically prohibits States from making anything except gold or silver coin legal tender in payment of debts. So, use it when you can – demand that all tax bills be paid with gold or silver coin – the States and counties consider a tax bill as a debt. Demand payment of obligations from the States in gold or silver coin. It would be very difficult to do this, but even a cursory effort will bring attention to the fact that the States are not conforming to the requirements of the U.S. Constitution. It is essential for the tail to stop wagging the dogs!

Gold has been used as a monetary or exchange unit for over 3,000 years. It was essential to keeping all the land barons and kings from just declaring rocks or sea shells to be legal tender. Often the value of gold was remotely connected to the cost of finding it, getting it out of the ground, refining it and then hammering or stamping it out as coinage. In order to protect their gold treasure, monarchs of old would often melt the stuff and make oversized ingots that raiders and other thieves would find difficult to move. One cubic foot of gold weighs over 1,200 pounds.

But then came the printing press – a banker's dream! While most people think of the invention of the printing press as related to books and newspapers, but the government controllers and bankers saw it as a means to expand the monetary system and increase their own wealth in the process. Here comes paper money, banknotes, green-backs, wampum, gold certificates or whatever designation the people would give it – but it was still just paper!

At first the bankers knew that if they wanted people to turn-in their heavy gold and silver coins for paper money, the bank would have to keep a lot of that gold in reserve in the event the people wanted the precious metal instead of banknotes. When the public became accustomed to doing their daily transactions with banknotes and felt reasonably secure about getting gold coins in exchange for the paper money, the bankers became greedy. Instead of just issuing bank-notes equal to the amount of gold they held, they started printing more notes and eventually were printing four and five times more paper money than they could possibly redeem in the event of a run.

All those private bank-notes created another problem – all banks weren't equal and a banker in Denver might not want to accept a note from a bank in Chicago or New York. That, plus the numerous runs on smaller banks, brought gold and paper money to the attention of the U.S. government.

The value established by Congress on U.S. gold coinage remained at $19.30 an ounce for 42 years and in 1834 Congress raised the price of gold to a whopping $20.67. It remained at the valuation for 100 years and the U.S. economy went through a civil war, built railroads across the plains, went through an industrial revolution and the expense of The Great War (WWI). But the private banks were still running rough-shod over their customers with varying exchange rates and those elected officials in Washington, DC, were constantly interfering with their financial deals. In 1907 a number of big bankers met at a place called Jekyl Island and laid-out the plans for a central bank – a banker's bank – the Federal Reserve. Congress and the U.S. Treasury Department were very receptive to the idea of a Central Bank to control all those independent bankers. The Federal Reserve was established and was relegated to buying only the Treasury Bills that Congress authorized. But some of those devious bankers were put in charge of the Federal Reserve and proceeded to adjust interest rates to compete with private bonds.

This, in turn, eventually resulted in Congress spending more money (inflation) and the public started taking risks in the stock market. Here comes the Great Depression!

Newly elected President Franklin D. Roosevelt (FDR) decided that even more money needed to be put in circulation and he encouraged Congress to raise the rate of an ounce of gold to $35. Ahhhh – more money to spend! Then, to make sure the people and bankers didn't sabotage his plans by using precious metals for commerce, FDR declared it illegal for anyone to have gold bullion or coins.

By 1973 international pressure was on the almighty American green-back and the dollar was devalued by raising the price to $42.22 for one ounce of gold. About that same time the dollar was allowed to "float" compared to gold and by 1975 it took $120 (fiat money) to buy one ounce of gold. Each time gold increased in price the dollar was devalued and inflation erupted – virtually stealing buying power from the people. But it wasn't the value placed on the gold - gold increased in value because government was spending money it created out of thin air, with nothing to back it up!

Inflation became a norm and over the 50-year period from 1964 to 2014, almost everything increased in price 10-fold: A newspaper or soft-drink that cost 10 cents in 1964 now costs $1.00. A new car that sold for $3,500 in '64 sold for over $35,000 in 2014. A loaf of bread was 21 cents and today it is about $2. Do the math – everything cost 10 times more! But the income of workers did not keep pace with that inflation. In 1964 the minimum wage was $1.25 - that would mean the minimum wage today should be $12.50.

CAN WE GO BACK?

Some economists say "no" and others say "yes"!

Returning to a Gold-Silver "Standard" is the only way to avoid repeats of the financial mess this nation (and the world) is presently facing. Call it a recession or a depression, the facts remain that government printing money or credits with nothing to back them up except a "promise" or a "trust in God" is similar to an individual running up a credit card with no job and no way to pay the bill when it is due. Like the government, a private citizen would just have to borrow more money to pay the interest on the money already owed.

According to Mrs. Bettina Bien Greaves, a financial scholar who writes on the subject of returning to the gold standard, it can be done! In her extensive writings on the subject Mrs. Greaves references the economic expertise of Hans F. Sennholz, Henry Hazlitt, Percy L. Greaves, Jr., and Ludwig von Mises.

"Certainly if the United States went on a gold standard, it would have to carry out many reforms. The federal government would *really* have to stop inflating, balance its budget, and abandon welfare state programs. Most voters are not ready for such reforms. And politicians, pressured by voters and special interest groups for favors, hesitate to pass them. Thus the major stumbling block to monetary reform is ideological. If this basic obstacle could be overcome, however, a return to gold money would become a realistic possibility," she writes.

But, like any problem situation, it can not be resolved in one great swoop. It takes planning and, since it took 100 years to get into our present financial mess, there is no reason to believe we can get out of it in less than 25 years – with planning.

CHAPTER 30
FIXING THE JURY
And The Justice System

So you received that notice: "Greetings: You have been selected for Jury duty!" Now, what do you do?

If you are like most people you start looking for ways to avoid this duty call. It is the duty of every citizen to serve on a jury when called. Having independent jurors to decide litigation, criminal and civil, is one of the bulkheads necessary to maintain liberty and justice for all. The problem is the jury systems, at every level, are time-consuming, frustrating and expensive.

In this day of technology, there is absolutely no reason for our jury system and the resulting justice(?) to be so unfair, cumbersome, delayed and lacking in justice that the average citizen will try and find a way to avoid serving on a jury. Answering the jury duty call for the first time and reporting to the court, as ordered, usually wakes up a person to the screw-ups that exist in our legal system of questionable justice.

Most of us have seen enough of those half-hour and 60-minute trial versions on television to know that lawyers have numerous gimmicks to ask for a "continuance" or a "recess" or the judge may order a meeting in his or her chambers. Each time this happens, you, as the juror, are left waiting in some room for the trial to continue – for minutes, hours and sometimes days. Even when court is recessed for several hours or days, you must be available to return when notified. Frustrating? You bet – and there is more!

After you did your duty and sat on that jury for a day or a week and your fellow jurors have heard the testimony and seen the evidence and are ready for final summations from the lawyers and instructions from the judge, the court could announce that the litigants have reached a settlement and your services are not longer needed by the court.

But wait! Maybe you and your fellow jurors did take the questions to the jury room and after due deliberation, you all agreed to find for or against the litigants and you announced your cumulative decision in open court! Or, as is sometimes the case, you and your fellow jurors disagree and a "hung-jury" results in a mistrial that will require going through the entire process with another jury. A very expensive process for the taxpayers, a waste of time for the courts, the witnesses, the litigants and everyone involved – but justice must be the outcome!

Keep in mind, almost everyone in that courtroom is being paid to be there – the lawyers, judge, court reporter, bailiffs and even some expert witnesses. If it is a criminal trial, the defendant usually isn't being paid to be in court. But in civil cases, even the plaintiff and defendant are betting that they will win and reap financial rewards. But you, the juror, are only paid a pittance.

And if all that isn't frustrating enough, you could have more frustration in store for you! After you made your decision, the court could set the jury's findings aside because it doesn't think one side or the other didn't do a satisfactory job of proving their points. Or the lawyers for the losing side appeals and your findings are reversed. Or the convicted criminal is given a "suspended sentence" for committing what you and your fellow jurors considered a heinous crime. Or an appeals court finds that the trial judge committed some error during instructions to the jury and the findings are set aside and a new trial is ordered!

Wasted time? Expensive procedures? Justice denied? The answer is "Yes!" - but it doesn't have to be that way!

The Real Fix For A System That Sucks!!

It would be difficult to fix the initial call to jury duty, but once this is accomplished and some juror excuses minimized, the wasted time and taxpayer expense can be cut considerably if the courts utilize current technology.

Some courts are already allowing video cameras in the courtroom, partially to reinforce the transcripts of the court reporters. But why should a properly impaneled jury have to waste so much time listening to objections and legal arguments that they are then told to "ignore" after the bell has been rung? What nonsense! The jury heard it and it doesn't make any difference what instructions the judge gives them – they heard it! Key witnesses die or can't be found? Case is down the drain! Wasted time! Years have elapsed since the event in question occurred and witnesses' memories are challenged. What nonsense!

Without a jury being present, why not just video every witness with both sides present and in front of the judge (in the courtroom) and just move matters along.

If an objection is made, the court rules, but the questions and proceedings continue as if no objection had been raised.

Each witness is brought in when available – not three years later! Their testimony is subject to the same questioning from counsel and it is in court, on video(s). It might be necessary to have four video cameras going at one time – one on the witness, another on the judge and still two more on the two tables for the litigants.

When all the evidence and testimony has been gathered on video, the litigants, lawyers and the judge get together to edit it. The objections raised can be reviewed by a higher court. If upheld, the objection and resulting questions and answer are deleted from the edited video. If the higher court finds that the question is reasonable, the objection is deleted and the answer is edited back into the final video. Testimony of a witness that improperly mentions something about the defendant's past indiscretions that would not be permitted by the court are automatically deleted. The "bell cannot be un-rung" and the "spilled milk cannot be put back in the bottle!" The final jury would never hear or see these legally inadmissible matters. The final video of all accepted witnesses, questions, answers, evidence (without objections, delays and arguments) will constitute the final case to be presented to the jury.

When all is said and done, the final video for what might have been a two-week trial with all the delays, could be reduced down to just a three hour presentation. The jury pool is questioned and told that if there is any reason they cannot devote three hours to watch the trial and whatever time it might take for deliberations, they "might" be excused. But how many people can honestly say they can't realistically put in three hours watching a real case on a giant TV screen? Most spend that much time watching idiot shows on TV and their favorite sports team play a game.

Then, later, if case is declared a mistrial or a higher courts find some error in the proceedings presented to the jury, the judge, lawyers and the litigants can go back to the video editing equipment, add or subtract whatever and empanel another jury to watch the 3 hour video and consider the case. No more witnesses, no expensive courtrooms. Savings to the taxpayers, the jurors and the confidence in our justice system would be tremendous!

A jury trial by our peers is very important to justice. But those peers can't just be a minority of people who are "available" because they are unemployed or retired - that is not sufficient. Too many qualified "peers" are being excused from jury duty - and that makes the present system SUCK!

The Internet is a great tool for informing the world!
If you are on the Internet with a website, blog or social media, get this information out.

THE AFTERWORD

While some citizens just go along and don't give more than lip service to the problems that exist in our system and government, others want to fix it. However, the fixes can't be accomplished over night. We are all on the same bus and at the speed our faltering system is going, we can't just whip a U-Turn to put us on the right path. That would flip the bus over!

America, and a good part of the free world, faces numerous problems involving jobs, business, homes, insurance, mortgages, energy, immigration and the list goes on! Most of us are aware of these problems but we only advocate treating each category as "the problem" rather than as "symptoms" of the real conditions.

It is somewhat like feeling run-down; no energy, numerous pains, swelling of various joints, mental depression and lack of ability to concentrate. We then take all those symptoms to the doctor. Unable to identify the root cause of the problems the medical profession gives it a name and declares it is a "syndrome". That's the tag given to symptoms when the experts can't identify the actual disease. Until the cause of the disease is determined, they can only treat the symptoms – a pill for this and a shot for that. Often the treatment makes the overall condition worse as the body tries to adjust for all the chemicals it is ingesting.

This is exactly what has been happening with our nation, our liberty and the economy. We could call it a "depression syndrome." To treat it the politicians and economists prescribe numerous pills and shots to get the economy going while libertarians demand a restoration of the Rights we lose as the experts keep handing out more pills to treat the symptoms.

It is essential that we determine the actual cause of the disease – the disease itself – and identify any individuals or groups who are "carriers" of the nation's sickness! A "carrier" may be an unsuspecting individual or organization or it could be some individual or corporate entity that actually profits from the spread of the disease.

Look back 30 or 40 years when the problems started to manifest themselves – back when our National Debt was doubling every 8 years or so. Our economy has always been subjected to ups and downs with a seemingly endless series of recessions, depressions and booms. While we let the economists and politicians declare the varying status of the economy to exist, we advocate only treating the symptoms that the economic disease has generated. This must change!

There are some valid arguments against positions taken in this book. One is the adage that we need some rules to live by — "Rules are the price we pay for living in a civilized society." To some extent that is correct. But will society allow someone to move out to a farm in the hinterlands and not harass them?

Those controllers, bureaucrats and rule makers cannot stand the idea of anyone being out of step and beyond their control. If you have a small farm, there is a government agency that will seek you out and try to coerce you into obeying their rules, pay taxes for their schools and build your cabin or outhouse according to their building code.

But consider that the planners for communities have

serious problems. How would you go about planning for a city which is expected to double in size from half-million to over 1 million people in just 10 years? Just the basic essentials of sewage and water, police and fire protection, traffic flow and minimal medical facilities — you cannot plan for such things, on that scale, without information and some type of controls.

The rules of a bureaucratic civilization must not be foisted on all segments of society. There must be a place in this nation where people can live un-harassed by controllers when they have had enough of society's rules, regulations and controls. If those who want to live free can actually find a place in this country to which they can escape and still remain free citizens, then the bureaucrats in the cities, counties, states and in Washington, D.C., can pass and enforce all the regulations their controlled residents will tolerate — provided they do not use threats, intimidation, fraud and trickery to get the people to unknowingly volunteer away their Rights!

Jay Evenson

Updates of Information and variations of the tricks being played are available on the Internet:

www.SFAmerica.net

YOUR INPUT and
QUESTIONS are
SOLICITED!

Contact SFA for Speaking Engagements and Talk Shows

INDEX

INDEX

U

U.S.D.A, (See Agriculture)
UNALIENABLE, 60
UNITED STATES CRIMINAL CODE, 93,
   203
URBAN DEVELOPMENT, 41, 49, 91
URBAN RENEWAL, (See HUD)
US-CFTA, 95 (See Free Trade)

V

VAGUE, 63, 64, 80, 148
VESSELS, Liability,112
VIETNAM, 68, 70
VOLENTI NON FIT INJURIA, 27, 45,
   121, 172
VOLUNTARY, Defined, 31
VON MISES, Ludwig, 230

W-Y

WASHINGTON, D.C., 11, 67, 82, 164, 182,
   213-215, 219, 220, 222, 229, 240
WEAPONS, (See Firearms)
WILLFUL, Define, 31, 207, 208
WORKER'S PERMIT CARD, 138

YOUNG v YOUNG, 31

:

:

www.ingramcontent.com/pod-product-compliance
Lightning Source LLC
Chambersburg PA
CBHW060353200326
41519CB00011BA/2128